PART 1
THE BACKGROUND

CHAPTER 1
WHAT IS THE POINT OF CONFIRMATION?

It's important, I think, that we understand what the point of confirmation is before we start to plan our preparation. What we do with our group, the things we share with them, the stuff we learn, will be different depending on what we think the service at the end of the preparation is there for.

In the training I do for dioceses, I suggest that we often have four things in mind when we talk about confirmation. I ask those present whether confirmation is a rite of passage, an initiation ceremony, a public declaration of faith or a sacrament.

Obviously the answer is 'Yes' to all the above! This fantastic service that we offer in the Anglican Church somehow manages to fulfil all the above roles. It's incredibly diverse, it serves a multitude of purposes – and that's great news. I think, though, that it's right to unpack each idea briefly and explore what impact it might have on the shape of the preparation we do with our young people.

A RITE OF PASSAGE

Adulthood is something to be celebrated! I know that's not fashionable – nobody seems to want to be a grown-up in the twenty-first century – but I think that as the Church we need to model a real concern for helping people embrace maturity. As a rite of passage, confirmation may lack some of the impact of a Jewish Bar Mitzvah or one of many other rites of passage, but it's the rite we've got, and we need to make the most of it. We'll talk in more detail about what it means to be a mature Christian in the next chapter – here I want to reflect on why it's important that we do celebrate with our young people as they take an adult step of faith.

Our culture deifies youth, sneers at 'growing up'. As a Church I believe we need to buck that trend – to love young people certainly and enjoy their energy and their creativity, but help them discover what it means to be a 'grown-up'. We need to celebrate maturity and encourage responsibility. At the same time we need to be careful how we communicate that to our young people. Tell them their confirmation is a chance for them to become proper Christian grown-ups and they may well run a mile – minds filled with people in patterned jumpers and open-toed sandals on caravan holidays.

In the collection *Through the Eyes of a Child*, 15-year-old Philip Fryar talks about his impressions of the adults he meets in church – people who didn't listen to him and only wanted him to sign up to their rather black-and-white views of the world, church and heaven.[1] Young people will want to embrace an adult Christianity but only if the adults they see in church look like the kind of people they want to be.

David Kinnaman devotes a major part of his book *You Lost Me* to a discussion of the six things young people suggest as their reasons for leaving church – or perhaps you could say the six attitudes exhibited by adult Christians that made them want to leave. Those Kinnaman spoke to saw Christian adults as overprotective, shallow, anti-science, repressive, exclusive and doubtless.[2] Of those six it's perhaps the frustration with a shallow faith that might surprise us the most. It's tempting to think that young people are after an easy life, rejecting anything that seems too hard or demanding. The media would certainly have us believe they're essentially lazy and uncommitted. But time and again Kinnaman met young people who were massively disappointed with the shallowness they saw exhibited by the adults they mixed with in church. Even more worryingly, it didn't seem to occur to many of these young people that their faith was meant to stretch out into the rest of the week.[3]

Confirmation can serve as an excellent rite of passage. In it we join with the bishop, and through him the rest of the Anglican Church, to support young people as they make solemn promises to live out their faith and the words spoken over them in baptism. Can we also make sure the adults they see in their church are living out the kind of faith that makes them want to take those promises seriously?

If a rite of passage is your main concern when preparing your group for confirmation, then you need to treat them as adults once they've been confirmed. It's no good holding confirmation up as this stepping-off point into adulthood if once they're confirmed they go back to the children's group to do more colouring in. We need to make an effort to speak to young Christians who've made an adult step of faith as if we really did think they were adults. We need to seek their opinions and their advice; we must plan services that help them feel involved and loved. We need to make sure we seek their input into the planning of the confirmation service itself. Their preparation must be serious, 'adult' stuff, with good theology, profound Bible knowledge and the challenge to live out a Christian faith marked by spiritual disciplines and patterns.

I'm currently doing a lot of work visiting deanery chapters around the Diocese of Winchester, meeting with clergy and encouraging them to be on the lookout for young people in their congregations and communities who may have some kind of ministerial vocation. I'm enjoying telling the story of the minister who looked at me at the age of 15 and told me he thought God might be calling me to ordained ministry. I didn't run a mile; I wasn't horrified at the thought that I might end up as a vicar. Rather I can remember the deep pride I felt that someone had noticed me, noticed my potential and had chosen to talk to me about it. When I look at the number of people in my youth group who are now in some kind of full-time ministry I can see that it was having our faith taken seriously that may well have led to so many of us stepping into a life of service. And while I have not, or not yet, gone down the ordination route, this year marks my seventeenth year in full-time Christian ministry. I'm convinced that young people will fulfil whatever expectations we have of them – if we expect them to grow into mature young adults, filled with the Spirit, dedicated to God, then there has to be a good chance that's what will happen.

AN INITIATION CEREMONY

While the language of 'initiation ceremony' sounds rather stark, at its most basic this is the human outcome of confirmation. The service at one level marks full membership of the candidate into the Anglican Church. On the face of it, the simple question is, 'So what?' I know very few young people who are even aware that they're Anglican, let alone passionately seek membership of that particular denomination. The majority of those I meet are content to be Christian, and any label beyond that is frankly immaterial. That's also the case for a large number of the youth workers I come into contact with. Many aren't from an Anglican background, and the practices of the Church of England are a mystery to them. Many young people may have youth workers who are at best indifferent about confirmation, and some actively discourage it, favouring adult baptism or reaffirmation of baptismal vows. It's even the case that many potential ordinands get a long way through the selection programme before 'fessing up' about their credentials. 'They just don't understand the Anglican Church' is something I regularly hear from the Diocesan Director of Ordinand's office!

This initiation aspect of confirmation really isn't something to avoid or be ashamed of. There's nothing wrong with being an Anglican. In fact to be a member of this vast organization, which welcomes people from all walks of life, of all church traditions and all theological backgrounds is something of an honour really. I for one love it. I love the fact that I'm part of a family – yes, we bicker and fight and sometimes fall out over things, but that's part of being family.

If we want our young people to take this whole 'adult faith' thing seriously, they need to be able to step into appropriate roles and responsibilities – I'd love to see them sitting on PCCs, taking their place on the preaching rota or the intercessions, serving the cup at communion. All these are vital to being part of the Church and all demand that young people sign up, become full members – get confirmed.

Furthermore, confirmation serves as a philosophical rite of initiation. It's not just jumping through legal hoops, it's about putting your name to something and saying, 'I agree with what this group stands for.' Young people are no strangers to tribes – the way they dress, the music they listen to and the way they speak will mark them out as being a member of a particular tribe. Confirmation is the way we say, 'I'm a part of the Anglican tribe', and that's a really exciting decision to make.

So if it's an initiation ceremony that you most desire for your young people, make sure they know they've joined something. Go crazy with the welcome party. Have hoodies made for them with your church name and 'Class of 2015' (or the relevant year) printed on the back. Invite them to meetings, to visit the PCC, to report to the APCM. Get them up front on Sunday morning after they've been confirmed to introduce them and welcome them to the church. Get them an inscribed Bible. Pay for them to visit your mission partners somewhere in the world! The options are pretty much endless – just make sure they know they've joined something bigger than themselves or their youth group.

A PUBLIC DECLARATION OF FAITH

For many young people, this seems to be the big one. There's something about standing up and publicly saying something that crystallizes it, makes it take shape and be real.

You don't have to dig very deeply into adolescent development theory to discover that it's unlikely that pre- and early adolescents will 'own a faith'. James Marcia is a clinical and developmental psychologist who's built on the work of Erik Erikson, the godfather of developmental psychology. Erikson argued that adolescence was the process of negotiating the 'crises' of our formative years and discovering our identity in the process. Marcia suggests that adolescents go through a stage of 'foreclosure' in their development – usually during pre-adolescence – characterized by an acceptance of the identity their family have chosen for them. For children who've grown up in a Christian family, this will characteristically be a 'blind' acceptance of the faith the parents have shared with them and the practices that go with it. The psychologists Douglas Kimmel and Irving Weiner observe that 'adults . . . are likely to praise foreclosed adolescents for their reliability, steadfastness and sense of purpose', while acknowledging that young people demonstrating the traits of foreclosure tend to make 'premature personal commitments as a way of skirting exploration and avoiding uncertainty'.[4] This is a hard pill to swallow, and I'm certainly not suggesting that young people's faith isn't real. It's more that only when they've weathered some of the crises of adolescence will they be able to hold a faith they've worked out for themselves. Evidence suggests that before this mid- to late-adolescent stage, children's beliefs are largely imitations of the faith they see around them, primarily from parents. It's why children with parents of no faith are so unlikely to discover God themselves, and why it's so important for adults in the church to model a faith that is attractive.[5]

I don't know about you, but I'm very much a verbal processor. I love ideas and I'm passionate about learning, but I need to talk something through – or at least write it down – for it to make sense. Let me give you an example. I recently met with the Bishop of Winchester for him to unpack some of the thoughts and vision he had for the diocese. He's a big thinker. Every room in the house is lined with books; he's an avid reader and a digester of ideas on a big scale. It can mean that a 20-minute discussion can feel like several theology lectures piled one on top of the other. My head was spinning by the time we'd covered Mission Action Planning, the Benedictine Rule of Life, N. T. Wright, Gerald Arbuckle, along with the proliferation of dark matter throughout the universe. I had all this information whizzing around and no obvious way to fit it all together. So I did what I do best – sat down and wrote a paper (I know how to live!). Needless to say, the activity of putting all those thoughts and reflections into some kind of coherent form helped the whole conversation make some kind of sense.

The confirmation service serves a similar kind of purpose, pulling abstract thoughts and reflections together into a concrete activity. For a young person who has a head full of questions, ideas and doubts, the act of standing and articulating quite clearly the core of his or her belief is an amazing moment. I remember a young person who told me that it was at the moment of confirmation that her faith 'took wings and flew'. In some senses that's why we make the event so grand. It's why the bishop is there (well, one of the reasons), it's why we invite our families and friends, why we take the preparation so seriously – all of this background stuff sets up the moment of declaration, the moment of 'This is what I believe'.

It doesn't solve all the problems or clear up all the questions, just as writing my paper didn't completely unpack the difference between dark matter and dark energy (answers on a postcard), but it does provide a kind of pivot, a moment on which an adolescent faith can turn.

If it's a public declaration of faith we want to maximize in our confirmation, there are plenty of ways we can make that our focus. Good preparation is a start – not so we can answer all the questions but so we can assure young people that the Christian faith is a reasonable faith, and that while doubts remain, we have a God in whom we can trust. Many confirmations allow space for candidates to share a little of their story as part of the service, which is a great thing to do, but even if that isn't possible, you can still invite your group to write to the bishop before the event and to tell him their story. Or you could encourage them to share their testimony in a Sunday service before or after the confirmation. It's simply about making opportunities for them to hang their own words on the decision they've made to get up in front of all those people.

A SACRAMENT

This final purpose of confirmation is perhaps the most difficult and the most exciting. The previous three cover the 'human activities' of confirmation. While God may work through and have a purpose for our activities of rites of passage, public declaration and initiation ceremony, the activity of the Spirit through it all isn't something we can create or control – 'The wind blows where it chooses' (John 3.8). We know that the Spirit will work and we trust that he will show up, but his activity is wonderfully out of our control.

I think we often get too hung up on the sacramental aspect of the confirmation service. I often joke when talking about confirmation that it's a 'sacrament' rather than a Sacrament. It's sacramental in as much as all activities can be sacramental – we can notice God in anything if we look, and in confirmation we can meet with God in a very real and very powerful way. I think this is distinct from a Sacrament – an activity ordained by Christ, a demand on us as followers of his way. For this reason I agree with the assertion in *On the Way*, the Church of England's 1995 report on Christian initiation, that there's an 'over-concentration of too much theology on one moment in the process'.[6] For that reason I don't want to enter into a long treatise on the workings of the Spirit and the theological process of initiation.

What I do want to say, however, is that the Holy Spirit does and will work at confirmation. When a bishop lays his hands on a believer's head, and prays for the coming of the Spirit – the Spirit comes!

While we can argue for the human aspects of confirmation, the importance of rites of passage and the life-marker placed by a public declaration of faith, to ignore the activity of the Holy Spirit would be foolhardy at best. The other reason young people find that their faith takes off at confirmation is because it's at that event that we prayed for them to be filled with the strengthening Spirit. It's why I'm really happy with the concept of the gift of the indwelling Spirit being given at baptism and the gift of the strengthening Spirit being given at confirmation. Does that mean the Spirit doesn't give strength to his children outside of that situation? Of course not. Again, the Spirit moves as he wills, but it does mean that we can expect something very special to happen at a young person's confirmation.

If we're keen to emphasize the sacramental nature of confirmation, how can we help a young person grasp that idea? Primarily we need to be talking about the work of the Spirit both in our preparation and in following up the event. Among many Christians there's still a lack of understanding about the Holy Spirit, and it can be particularly hard to discuss the Spirit with young people. They can grasp the concrete illustrations of Father and Son, but the Spirit, by nature, is a more abstract idea to come to terms with. We need to remember that as adults we can grasp the abstract, but for children this is far more complicated – the part of their brain that can handle the abstract literally hasn't developed yet. The developmental psychologist Jean Piaget called it the 'formal operational' stage, which begins in adolescence, when our brains start to develop the ability to work in the abstract.[7]

Helping pre- or early adolescent children have a concept of the workings of the Holy Spirit at Confirmation can be very difficult. We will in all likelihood end up talking about feelings, which is awkward because the risk is that they'll grow up thinking the Holy Spirit is all about making them feel good. It might be worth focusing on good concrete illustrations – for example, you could talk about Joshua standing on the edge of the promised land and his prayer that the Israelites would be strong and courageous (Joshua 1.7). This, you could explain, is a bit like what the Holy Spirit does at confirmation – he gives you the strength and courage that you'll need to move forward in following Jesus.

With older young people, we can still talk about feelings but we can also discuss why that's not the be all and end all. Explore with them stories from the Bible of what happens when the Spirit moves, unpack the strange warmth and confidence that comes from his presence, reflecting on people such as John Wesley who wrote about this experience of God at work. Explore concepts of God always being with us and around us, but balanced with at times deliberately coming into his presence. You may even want to sow an expectation in them that at confirmation the Spirit may move in quite remarkable ways.

As I said at the start of the chapter, we must really expect confirmation to fulfil a variety of purposes and not try to limit its appeal. In my view it's better to make the most of the tools the Church has given us, squeezing all the goodness out of them and even then waiting expectantly to see if God will do something else quite *un*expected.

CHAPTER 2
WHAT DOES IT MEAN TO BE AN ADULT CHRISTIAN?

The question I'd love to be able to answer for church leaders, above all others, is: 'How do we know when young people are ready to be confirmed?' It's a really difficult one, and certainly not something that has, in any way, a simple answer. I'm sure none of us would think we hit a certain age at which all of us are ready to be confirmed, but it's the practice we use in most of our churches. We tend to work to the academic calendar, and when young people reach a certain age we offer them the opportunity to get confirmed. Usually all it takes is one young person to say 'Yes' and a cohort will follow. As a rule we don't insist on confirmation and, ironically, those who decide they want to wait when their friends are all saying 'Me, please' are the ones we identify as having the most maturity.

As we prepare our groups we usually notice all manner of levels of maturity – the group of young people who sit and giggle, the individual who concentrates and takes notes on everything we say, the forest of hands, desperate to answer every question we ask.

When it comes to the big day, in our heart of hearts we know that while some of those we present to the bishop have developed a real and growing faith, others are simply along for the ride, and we simply have to entrust them to God. These are often the ones who come back some years later, concerned that they should have waited to get confirmed and seeking some new outward sign of the transformation they've experienced. They grumble that confirmation didn't mean anything and find a church that will offer them some kind of 'believer's baptism' or 'wet reaffirmation of baptismal vows'.

Add into that the pressure on many young people from mums and dads – or more often grandparents – to get confirmed, as well as a desire to do what an older sibling did two or three years ago, and the decision on when it's right to confirm becomes a minefield.

So how do we discern when someone is ready? On one level, we can't. Only God can know what's going on at the heart level in any one of us. It's why, despite writing in previous work on adolescent development, and making a case for holding off on confirmation until late adolescence,[1] I entirely understand why sometimes we confirm children at a much younger age. I remember very clearly when a child came to us at the age of ten and explained about the time she spent each day in prayer and Bible study. She told us about how she shared her faith with her friends and even articulated something of her understanding of vocation. Despite all my knowledge of child development and the place of confirmation in faith development, there was no way I or the vicar in the parish could deny this girl's request to be confirmed.

For me the key word, really, is discernment. Because while the youth worker in me screams that we need to let children and young people make their own choices and decisions, and while I'm absolutely convinced that the kingdom of God belongs to such as these, I'm also aware that Christian leadership means making decisions and taking a lead. Our decisions may not always be popular, and that's why leadership must always be based on relationship, so that children, young people and parents will know that when we make a decision they can trust it.

A THEOLOGY OF LEADERSHIP

I want to start by offering a theology of leadership. We live in a culture that appears to have issues with authority and leadership. Our political leaders have never been held in such low esteem, church leadership is constantly questioned by secular culture (often for good reason when we hit the headlines for all the wrong reasons), and young people are encouraged to stand up and question those in authority over them – teachers, the police and parents alike.

To offer leadership in such a time as this is a pretty daunting prospect, and so in many of our churches we find ourselves nervous of standing up and declaring the way forward for fear of rejection and ridicule. I regularly hear cries for leadership within the Church, usually followed by mutterings of disapproval when that leader makes an unpopular decision.

In the leadership of young people I am the first to call for them to be allowed to make their own decisions, to assess the facts and the evidence and to choose for themselves what it means to be a Christian and how to live that out. But I hold that in tension with the need for leadership. It's another – and there are many – 'now-and-not-yet' of the kingdom. We need to allow young people to find their own way but also to acknowledge that they need to be led and supported.

There are no end of books offered on good leadership – many written from a business perspective – that urge us to confident, decisive leadership. Many echo the mantra coined by former US Secretary of State, James Baker, in 2001: 'leadership is knowing what needs to be done... and getting it done'. Reading a Pauline theology of leadership can easily reinforce those strong leadership images. According to Paul, leadership is a gift from Christ himself (Ephesians 4.11; Romans 12.8), designed for a clear hierarchy (1 Timothy 3). Our leaders' authority is further promoted by Paul's encouragement to the rest of us to submit (Hebrews 13.17).

It's not surprising, then, that books like *Developing a Theology of Leadership* by Tony Morgan can teach that 'not all of us are leaders. Although everyone can learn leadership skills, not everyone is gifted to be a leader.'[2]

While there's a theological strength to these kinds of arguments, I think they fall way short of a full biblical picture of leadership. In the *Gospel and the Catholic Church*, the former Anglican Archbishop Michael Ramsey asserted that any theological view of leadership needs to be framed within the context of Christ.[3] Any leadership we exert over the followers of God only happens within the context of a Church that is the body of Christ, and Christ was and is our ultimate model of leadership. And so these triumphal modes of leadership with at least one foot firmly planted in the world of business need to stand against the example of the servant king as he knelt on the floor and washed the dirt from his disciples' feet. The strong, visionary leader has to sit at the feet of the God who 'made himself nothing by taking the very nature of a servant' (Philippians 2.7 NIV).

So how do we hold that tension? How do we hold the Pauline picture of leadership in one hand and the Christological picture of the leader as servant in the other? For me the answer lies in relationship. In youth work it's an image we learn very early on. Our relationship with young people is entirely voluntary. They choose to have a relationship with us and we must earn the right to have that relationship. The sign that we've achieved the best we can in a relationship with young people is when they give us permission to challenge their behaviour, but that process takes time, starting from the initial nod as we pass them on the street, through to giving them opportunities to be members of youth councils and leadership committees. If I have a good understanding of relational youth work, then I know that because of the time and diligence I've put into building a relationship with a young person, I've earned the right to challenge his or her decision when it comes to the question: 'Should I get confirmed or not?'

Often, though, it's not the youth leader who gets to help make that choice, and with the best will in the world a member of the clergy who's had little to do with the young person until the point of confirmation preparation should be nervous about deciding whether or not that person is ready. In the context of good relationship, a church leader can sit and talk with the family and have the kind of robust conversation that leads to a positive decision for everyone.

Put simply, we don't need to question whether we have the authority to help people decide whether or not they're ready for confirmation, provided we've first put in the work of building the kind of relationships where we have permission to have those kinds of conversations.

There are of course always going to be situations in which strangers or relative strangers approach us to explore confirmation, whether in a school where we don't know the parents especially well or a parish church where the vicar gets a call out of the blue from a parent whose child wants to be confirmed. I would suggest that just as a family seeking baptism or a couple wanting to get married would be expected to first spend some time becoming part of the family, we could recommend this for a prospective confirmation candidate and thus start the process of building that kind of permission-giving relationship we desire.

DISCIPLE VS DISCIPLESHIP

The language of disciple and discipleship are daily fare for us in the Church at the moment. Everything we do seems to be geared towards making and growing disciples. Yet I'm not convinced we always necessarily know what that means. I think we can be fairly sure what some of the signs of discipleship are, but trying to define what a disciple is – beyond being 'a follower of Jesus' – is much harder.

There are plenty of models and pictures available to help us understand where someone is on his or her discipleship journey. The Engel scale is probably one of the best known, marking a 'spiritual awareness' scale that moves from –7 ('No real awareness [of God]') to +4 ('Growth in Christ'). The zero point is marked as the 'Decision' moment – a classic evangelical picture of the moment when one 'prays the prayer' and becomes a Christian.[4]

It would be nice if we could line young people up against the Engel scale, make a note of where they are and then decide that once they've passed the zero point, we know they're ready to be confirmed and we can sign them up. Wouldn't it be fantastic if Jesus had modelled this for us 2,000 years ago! The trouble is that life is far messier than that, and discipleship far more complicated. It's very rare anyone follows some linear journey through discipleship to Christ.

An activity I regularly use with young people illustrates this perfectly. Often at the start of confirmation preparation I'll stick a big sheet of paper to the floor and place a candle at the centre. I ask everyone to imagine the candle represents Jesus, the light of the world. I give each a pen and invite them to draw a path that represents their journey towards Christ, taking into account the highs and lows, the times they felt close to him and the times they felt distant. Needless to say, I've never seen anyone draw a dead straight line towards the candle. Rather, by the time the activity is over it looks as though a bunch of snails have had one too many hits of communion wine and then weaved their way drunkenly across the paper. In fact I usually do the activity with the group, and my path is as drunken-looking as the rest of them.

That's why, while they have their uses, diagrams and scales such as Engel's are too tidy for real life. I'm not sure I'm even convinced by the 'moment' of becoming a Christian. Don't get me wrong: I know plenty of Christians who can tell you the day and time when they made their commitment to Christ. They can point to the event when they heard a gospel message, knew it was true and responded. My suspicion, though, is that that moment was probably part of a greater process of learning and discovery. There seem to be far more Nicodemuses than Pauls in my experience.

When I was studying at King's College, London, my course tutor Pete Ward spent some time helping us think through that moment of salvation. He used the worship time at Soul Survivor[5] as his illustration. His question was complex: if some young people spend 40 minutes worshipping in God's presence with the Soul Survivor band, feeling his power working in their lives; and then listen to a gospel talk where their eyes are opened and they discover the truth about Christ; and then respond to the call to the front to be prayed for and ministered to; and then go out the back to meet with a leader who'll take them through a prayer of commitment – at what point did they 'become Christians?'

If that process had got interrupted for some reason, how far would they have had to go before they'd crossed the 'zero point' on Engel's scale?

I'm conscious that I'm splitting hairs a little here, but if that process had been stretched out as it is for most of us, with the 40 minutes of worship spread over years of wonder and awe at the world we live in; the gospel talk split across dozens of sermons, readings, Bibles passages, conversations; the 'call to the front' marked by lots of little commitments to get involved (helping out at Messy Church, giving out books, cooking for an event and the prayer of commitment); an Alpha course, confirmation course or a few years of catechism, then the question becomes more relevant.

How do you mark the before and after? How do you decide whether someone is in or out? It's fabulously complicated.

BELONG, BELIEVE, BEHAVE

There are some talks, I'm sure you'll agree, that just stay with you. I can remember so clearly, as a teenager, listening to Steve Chalke talking about the mix-up we had in the Church about discipleship and the challenge we faced if we truly wanted to be the kind of place people wanted to be a part of.

The issue, he explained, drawing on the work of Grace Davie,[6] was that in many of our churches we expect people to behave a certain way before we'll let them belong to our group. If our churches are only really accessible to people of a certain intellect and with a certain way of dressing and speaking, then the pool of those who'll be welcome is going to be pretty small. And really it's in belonging that I'll discover the chance to believe. It's in belonging that I'll discover the relationships and the prayer and the teaching that will illuminate Christ for me and give me something to believe in. In fact I'm unlikely to believe *until* I belong!

Steve Chalke's critique of a Church that insisted on people behaving correctly and believing the correct stuff before they could belong has had a huge impact on me. It's revolutionized the way I view discipleship. Chalke suggested that a better model – arguably Jesus' model – is the expectation that people will *belong* then *believe*, and that in turn their *behaviour* will be affected. I want to address belonging and believing before moving on to behaviour.

I think that in terms of youth work we've pretty much got our heads around this idea of belonging. We've talked about relational youth work for long enough that it's become the norm. I can't remember the last time I saw youth work that didn't involve some kind of food or work hard to provide space for young people to come and be. In fact this whole book is written on that premise – that learning is something that grows out of belonging and relationship rather than a 'You sit; I speak; you learn' kind of model.

That doesn't mean we've got it made. Young people are fiercely tribal, deeply suspicious of people who aren't like them. I've worked in youth groups that needed to be split into two separate nights – one for those who dressed in black, one for those who mostly wore sportswear – and in settings where, once the local kids from the estate started attending, the church kids all left. On a recent visit to a youth group I was frankly quite disturbed by the attitude of the nice Christian young people I was chatting to towards the 'different' young man who came to join the table. But as far as modelling a kind of group where relationship is at the core, I think we're doing pretty well.

It follows that if we're encouraging young people to 'belong' first, then confirmation is an obvious symbol of that. Confirmation is, as we've discussed, a sign that we're members – that we've joined the Anglican Church. Surely then we should be offering confirmation to every teen who comes through the door?

If you're shrinking back at this point, don't worry – so am I, because confirmation *is* about membership, about belonging, but also about more than that. To focus purely on the belonging aspect of it is to deny the sacramental and rite of passage aspects of the service that I discussed in Chapter 1. It's about belonging, and about more than that too.

So if confirmation is about more than belonging, perhaps we need to wait until young people believe before they can be confirmed. That's fraught with danger too. What do we expect them to believe? And how deeply? What should be wrapped up? And what's still all right for discussion? It's really not straightforward. My seven-year-old daughter will probably never believe in God more strongly than she does right now – and I want to celebrate that. But her adult faith will have a different kind of richness to it, tested by the crises of adolescence and self-discovery – and I want to celebrate that too!

CHARACTER VS BEHAVIOUR

There's a fragment of a verse from Proverbs that I return to time and again: 'for though the righteous fall seven times, they rise again' (Proverbs 24.16 NIV). It seems there's something 'righteous' about the journey, about stumbling and getting back up, about failing but brushing oneself down and getting back on with it. I know there's also plenty of stuff about purity and holiness in the New Testament, plenty of behaviour stuff I feel challenged by on a daily basis. But the thing that gives me hope is the knowledge that if I keep on keeping on, somehow that's a godly thing.

The language of the Commission in the confirmation service really helps us here I think. It talks about *continuing* and *persevering*, *returning* and *seeking*. These all seem to be active, moving ideas – they're not stationary positions that we achieve.

I've always worried about the third part of the cycle Steve Chalke talked about – behaviour. While I agree we don't only want to welcome correctly behaving people into our churches, I'm concerned that somehow the pinnacle of discipleship is 'good behaviour'. It sounds rather school-like. My concern is that maybe we expect that if a young person is practising good behaviour, everything else will fall into place. Kenda Creasy Dean warns that 'practices do not transform us; *grace* transforms us'.[7]

I can't get excited about a youth ministry that exists to mould young people's behaviour. And while we might think that producing clean-living, upstanding young people is no bad goal, it sounds rather hollow.

I'd rather be involved in the work of young people growing in character, becoming wiser, more determined, more questioning – of faith, the world, their own actions. If that good character leads to 'good' behaviour, all well and good. I'm reminded that the religious people continually criticized Jesus for his behaviour – doing things that didn't sit right with their world view. It makes me very nervous about judging someone else's behaviour.

But if what we're seeking is the character of a disciple, then I think we're on to something. Let's think about the original disciples for a moment. You could argue that Pentecost was their confirmation moment – a bit of a reach, but stick with me. And if that's the case, we need to look at their character before that moment as something of a measure for our young people.

When we look at the pre-Pentecostal disciples we can probably understand why it is that so many people think Jesus' first followers were probably quite young. They argued about importance, they slept when they were meant to be praying, one of them even disowned Christ in response to peer pressure.

But they were also keen and committed. They wanted to please and serve this wonderful man who gave three years of his life to leading and mentoring them. Peter encapsulates that youthful exuberance for Christ that I sometimes wish I felt more often. The first time we meet him (Matthew 4.18) he literally drops everything to respond to the call of Christ. He steps out of the boat to join Jesus walking on the water (14.29). I love it when he leaps out of the boat and splashes to the shore to meet Jesus on the beach (John 21.7). And it's Peter, of course, who makes that wonderful pronouncement about Jesus being 'the Messiah, the Son of the living God' (Matthew 16.16).

Peter, it seems, was ready for confirmation because of his character – he was passionate about seeking Jesus, about learning about him, discovering what he had in store for him. He followed and trusted even when he didn't understand. And he screwed up – spectacularly sometimes. His behaviour was all out of sorts but his character was wonderful – and so Jesus declared that 'on this rock I will build my church' (Matthew 16.18 NIV).

Presented with a young Simon Peter, I wonder if we'd have considered him ready to be confirmed?

HOW DO WE KNOW THEY'RE READY?

And so we return to our opening question: How do we know if young people are ready to be confirmed? Our decision isn't going to be made by measuring prospective candidates against any scales. We're not going to be able to judge that at age X they're all set. But through relationship with them and their families we'll be able to help them make the right decision. Ultimately it's not really going to be up to us. We'll present them to the bishop, having done all we can to say in good conscience that they're ready. But it's through confidence in our leadership and through the knowledge we've gleaned through committing ourselves to good relationships that we'll be able to help them and their families make the right decision for themselves.

CHAPTER 3
A TYPICAL SESSION OUTLINE

At the risk of becoming boring, I need to re-emphasize the importance of how confirmation preparation is going to be different for your group from how it is for any of the groups I've run. Your group, this year, is probably different from the one you ran last year and completely different from the one in a neighbouring parish, let alone at the other end of the country. That's why the material in this preparation is meant to be a *guide*. What follows are some ideas that I hope will get your creativity flowing and provide space for your group to explore for themselves this mystery that we call the Christian faith. No matter how carefully I craft these sessions and no matter how tried-and-tested the ideas are (and they have been!), some will stick for you and others you'll reject out of hand. I'm part of a group that runs a Messy Church in my home parish. As a group we try, test and create many of the ideas that then go on to be published in the Messy Church books. I also run quite a lot of Messy Church training events, and more than once have had people tell me they'd use the ideas that are published but 'Let's be honest, some of them are pretty terrible!' I usually have to bite my tongue and swallow a little pride because I know the ideas worked at the Messy Church where I serve, and there's an outside chance I was involved in coming up with some of the ideas being critiqued! It means that writing any kind of guide like this has to be done with no small amount of humility.

So here's a session outline that I've found helpful. I'll explain the reasoning behind each step as we go so that you can see what the thought process is. (Here I don't discuss the short **Introduction** and **Learning outcomes** sections you'll find in each session in Part 2 as these are self-explanatory.)

SET THE SCENE

Before you start with the programme, it's worth spending some time on getting the ambience right wherever you plan to meet. The idea of confirmation preparation is to give young people the space and opportunity to open up about their faith, to explore what they believe and to be able to come clean about some of their doubts and questions. To make that as easy as possible, it's worth creating a space where those kinds of conversations can flow. Sitting in a cold church, in rows, with the leader standing at the front teacher-like, is unlikely to produce an atmosphere conducive to the kind of conversation we want to encourage.

Confirmation preparation somehow needs to feel special, so it's worth meeting somewhere that has that feel to it. While I don't remember much about the content of my confirmation preparation, I do remember that it took place in the chaplain's living room. To me it felt like a real privilege to be in this special place. It was in someone's home and somewhere I didn't usually get to visit. At the school where I regularly lead confirmation preparation we get to use the staff common room, a space usually out of bounds to students but open to them for these eight weeks of the year. This may be harder in a church setting, especially if your group is big, but if possible it's worth trying to meet somewhere warm and welcoming rather than in a hall or church building.

If you have no choice but to meet in a big room, do all you can to make the space feel smaller – beanbags or cushions in a circle can shrink a space, or rugs or throws on the floor can mark out a special area. Soft lighting with lamps can also add an air of intimacy.

It's also worth getting away at times if at all possible, especially if you're thinking about specific issues. If you want to wonder at God's creation, get outdoors and have a look at it. If you want some kind of retreat, go away for the day to a whole new setting. If you want to have some kind of preparation service (there's a suggested liturgy in Part 3), try to find a chapel or a setting that will help you set the right scene. When I got engaged I took my then fiancée out for a meal to celebrate. As we were young and skint, a meal at a Harvester restaurant seemed like a real treat. Needless to say I can remember the children's party at an adjacent table far better than what I ate or the conversation we shared. The wrong atmosphere definitely had a detrimental effect on that event!

OPENING WORSHIP

One of the biggest struggles with any youth meeting is trying to get past the idea that it's a social event with a God bit tacked on. In the early days of my youth ministry we used to have youth clubs with a 'God slot'. It's no wonder we always had a discipline issue during these times – the group felt aggrieved that we were trying to slot God into their fun and games. What's more it gave entirely the wrong message about our faith – we were saying to them, albeit by implication, that God could be slotted into life rather than being central or core, the main event if you like.

That's why during confirmation preparation I like to start with **Opening worship**. Don't panic – I'm not suggesting a lengthy liturgy or that you need to dust off your guitar and start singing songs (although if your group is up for that, go for it!). Instead I simply want to suggest some simple worship activities that might help you set the scene, help make it clear that everything you do together, whether a silly game, slices of pizza or a YouTube clip, is *all* the 'God bit'.

Below are several different worship activities you can do together – they're all very simple and mostly borrow from traditional or ancient worship practices. None of them requires any musical skill although as I say, if your group enjoys singing and you have the wherewithal to lead some kind of musical worship, you can weave that into your worship time. It's up to you how many of the worship activities you use – there's a really strong argument for repetition, and finding something your group engages with and then reusing it week in week out can be a really interesting activity. I've actually found with worship activities that used enough times, members of your group will be comfortable leading the worship themselves, which is a great skill to start developing in them.

In each of the following sessions where you are prompted to lead some **Opening worship**, you can either use the idea suggested in the session or refer back to this section of the book and choose which activity suits the theme or your group.

A BUNCH OF WORSHIP ACTIVITIES

CENTRING

The centring prayer is a very simple way of helping your group set aside the thoughts and the worries of the day and to focus in on God and on spending some time with each other and with him. I've quoted Mark Yaconelli's centring prayer in a previous book, but it bears repeating here.

Encourage your group to close their eyes and to sit quietly for a short while – for some this may be 5 seconds; others may manage 30 or more! Then quietly read these words:

> Imagine that you are walking down a staircase that begins in your mind and winds slowly down to your heart. Take a few moments to imagine walking this staircase, leaving all the many worries and thoughts behind, slowly descending into a secret room or chapel within your heart, where God waits to pray with you.[1]

Allow the group time to sit in quiet and then gently invite them to come back to the room, ideally before fidgeting sets in.

BREATHING

This is another exercise from Mark Yaconelli's book, again well worth repeating here.

Once again invite the group to sit quietly and allow them to relax and find a little bit of peace.

Close your eyes and simply notice your breathing. Take a moment to imagine the air in the room is filled with God's light and God's love. For the next few minutes just pay attention to your breathing, imagining with each in-breath that you are breathing in God's love and with every out-breath, that you are releasing every distraction, every anxiety, every tension and resistance to God.[2]

Allow the group to sit in quiet and when you judge they've had long enough, invite them to open their eyes and rejoin the session.

CANDLE/UPPER ROOM

This is possibly the simplest of all the **Opening worship** ideas and one I've used countless times with groups. It works particularly well because you can light a candle that can then burn throughout the session, reminding the group that they began their time together acknowledging God's presence. There'll inevitably be a fight for who should light the candle, so be prepared if you don't want this to be a big distraction!

Invite the group to stand around an unlit candle and read these words from Scripture, lighting the candle at an appropriate moment as a reminder of Christ's presence with you all.

Later on that day, the disciples had gathered together, but, fearful of the Jews, had locked all the doors in the house. Jesus entered, stood among them, and said, 'Peace to you.'

(John 20.19 THE MESSAGE)

Allow a short time of quiet and focus on the candle before continuing with your session.

BUSY HANDS

In my experience, if you want to get young people engaged in conversation and in a place where they're happy to open up, it's worth giving them something to do. Whether it's eating food, doing craft or going for a walk, I think we all talk easier when we're occupied.

Each of the sessions will have some opening questions – things for you all to talk about to get the subject going and everyone thinking. Rather than just outlining a bunch of questions for you to ask (which might feel a little false or sterile), I suggest you choose an activity from the ideas below and then ask the questions while the group is occupied. For most of us the activity will be as simple as sharing food together, and if that's how you start then I suggest you have food available at each subsequent meeting, even if you want to use a different **Busy hands** activity. A young person denied cake or pizza can be a dangerous thing . . .

Again, choose an activity you think your group will resonate with and will enjoy, but try not to do anything so complicated it precludes discussion. There are several ideas below, and each session in Part 2 will have a specific idea that will help you unpack that meeting's particular theme.

SOME 'BUSY HANDS' ACTIVITIES

FOOD

If all else fails, simply sit down and eat together. Sharing pizza is practically a cliché for youth work, but frankly it's still the best option there is for allowing space for your group to talk and discuss. You can do something simple like sandwiches or cake, whack a couple of pizzas in the oven or go for a different meal each week, travelling the world via local takeaways!

A WALK

Going for a walk is definitely another great way to loosen tongues. This may not be appropriate every week, but occasionally heading outdoors for a stroll can be a great activity. Some of your group may not be used to walking regularly, so this can feel like a real treat. Invite them to notice things as you travel – to spot what's going on, to see evidence of God or signs of injustice and need. Have challenges as you wander to spot or collect specific things. And chat! It's perfect!

CRAFT

Throughout this guide various craft ideas are suggested, but if you have something specifically that you enjoy, why not incorporate it? And don't be frightened of the boys not wanting to get involved – chosen carefully, craft activities can involve everyone.

BUILDING/FIXING PROJECT

If you're feeling particularly brave, set yourself a bigger challenge – start each of your meetings with an hour working on a big-scale project – doing up a car, fixing bikes, building a PC from scratch or even some kind of decorating project. As well as giving you space to chat, you might discover that the ongoing nature of the idea will attract your group back week after week – and maybe even give you an excuse to keep meeting after confirmation.

YOUTUBE OF THE WEEK

If nothing else, simply have a daft clip from YouTube to start your session with, especially if time is short. There are no end of funny cats, sneezing pandas and people falling over that will keep your group entertained, and if you can fit it into the message for the session, even better! It's worth nominating someone to suggest the YouTube of the week each week. Group members can take turns, though from experience they'll need plenty of reminding.

THE BIBLE BIT

Reading the Bible is a central part of discipleship. It's God's word for us; it endures; it teaches.

It's also hard. While parts of the Bible contain the most beautifully crafted prose, other sections are simply not written in that style and so can be much more difficult to access. What's more, the young people we're leading are part of a culture that has largely set books aside – how many of them breathe a sigh of relief when a book is made into a film because it means they don't have to bother reading any more! For many of us, reading is limited to catching up with friends via Facebook or Twitter, or it's something we have to do because of work, school or college. And while lots of us might devour a light, fluffy novel, we're less likely to be reading non-fiction books.. And let's be honest: the Bible hardly fits into the chick-lit genre.

So during our confirmation preparation we need to find ways to help our group engage with the Bible, learn how to read it, explore the mysteries hidden in it and appreciate it for what it is – God's word for us both today and throughout history.

You'll need to gauge how your group will get the best out of the Bible. Some will be very happy to read lengthy passages and to chat about what they've discovered. Others will prefer to read smaller chunks and examine each word in more detail. For some, just a Bible verse each week will be as much as they can manage. Find out what works best and go with it.

Each of our sessions will give you three **Bible-bit** options. The first is a long passage – one or several chapters – that your group can wrestle with together and then take home and read between sessions. You might want to give them the passage for the following week and get them all to read it ahead of time. Most groups will probably want to go for the middle option of a short passage that you can read together in the group, and which some can read and re-read in the intervening days. And third there's the option of a single Bible verse for those groups that will struggle with anything longer. You could encourage your group to learn the verse if you think they'd appreciate that opportunity – something you can reinforce with social media and text messages.

Following the Bible reading there'll be a series of questions. It's important to remember that for the most part these aren't questions with correct answers – this isn't a Bible comprehension exercise! Rather they're questions for you – and your group – to think about and discuss. You may need to give direction sometimes but it's important to remember at this stage that you're discovering the Christian faith together – you'll be amazed what you learn as you listen to your group talking about what they've heard.

WAYS OF READING THE BIBLE

Below are some suggestions for how you might like to get the most out of reading the Bible together, but again feel free to try all the ideas or, if you prefer, find one method that resonates and stick with it for all your sessions.

LECTIO DIVINA

If I could recommend just one method of reading the Bible to try week in week out with your group, this would be it. Lectio Divina – literally 'Holy Reading' – is an ancient method of Bible reading, and it's enjoyed quite a renaissance in recent years. There are plenty of detailed explanations of what to do and expect from Lectio Divina,[3] but at its core is the very simple practice of reading and rereading a text, expecting God to reveal something to you. Plenty of people use it in their personal reading, but I've found it to be excellent in a group setting.

You'll need to get your group settled and to choose three confident readers – members or leaders – who will lead the time. Explain that each person is going to read the passage through once and that you're all going to pause and think between each reading. Explain that when we hear the same words repeated we often hear words or phrases that catch our attention and make us think – I sometimes say it's like something scratching at the inside of your brain. So encourage the group to think 'What caught my attention?' between each reading.

Once the passage has been read for the third time, pause once more and then move into the questions for that session. You'll notice that every session starts with the same two questions: 'What caught your attention from these words? (Why?)' and 'What do you think God might be trying to get us to notice?' This is done so that if you choose to, you can use the Lectio Divina reading method at every session. This is what I've done with my groups in the past and have always found it useful. Occasionally the session may suggest a different way to read Scripture together – as ever I leave it to your discretion how you choose to work with your group.

DRAMATIZED

If your group is particularly into drama, brilliant – really go for it with a dramatized reading. Otherwise simply share out the voices and narration and get people involved. You can get specific dramatized versions of the Bible, but just using different voices throughout the reading can really change the way you listen.

SPLIT INTO CHUNKS

Even just splitting the passage down into two or three sections can make a difference. Encourage more than one person to have a go at reading, and keep the passage flowing. This is particularly good for getting everyone involved, even those who are nervous about reading out loud and might be happier just having a few words to read.

VIDEO

If you or someone in your group is into creating videos, you can go to town a bit here. Each week have films of the passage being read, made by a variety of people on a variety of locations. It needn't be overly complex and can probably be done in one take, which will save hours of editing time. Young people are drawn to screens and you can capitalize on this by putting the Bible on one – it will also benefit those members who learn best visually. If video is too difficult you can make a simple audio recording of the reading, again by choosing different voices to contribute and then playing the recording back to your group when you gather.

MUSIC

One of the simplest ways to add depth to the reading is to play music during it. Choose something quiet and preferably without lyrics, and play it as you or a member of the group reads. To emphasize: make sure the music is quieter than the reader – you don't want to lose the words!

NOTICING GOD

I'm very grateful to the Sticky Faith initiative from the Fuller Youth Institute in the USA, which has helped me rethink this particular section of the meeting. I struggle with prayer – I make no secret of it. I don't disagree with it (of course!), and I'm always in awe of Christians who can find the words to say to God when they sit down to make conversation with him. But for me it's always been difficult. What the Sticky Faith people have done is encourage me to rethink prayer as noticing God – looking for him in everything I do; wondering what he might be saying to me in different situations; trying to figure out what he is trying to teach me. Don't get me wrong: talking to God is vital – I need to learn to communicate with him, and we'll be doing plenty of that during our time together. But when so much human-to-human conversation is non-verbal – two-thirds according to the entry on non-verbal communication on Wikipedia[4] – it seems obvious to me that our prayer life, our communication with God, is likely to be equally non-verbal.

Some of the sessions will have specific prayer activities outlined in them because there are some subjects that will benefit from a particular prayer response, but for the most part it's again a case of choosing the activities you think your group will benefit from, and then either repeating your preferred activity or picking and choosing from a short list.

You might also want to choose between praying together as a group or finding ways of helping your group notice God throughout the week. Sometimes you might find that a simple closing prayer is just a good way to finish your time together – something as simple as saying the grace together will probably do. At other times, if the content of your time together has been particularly emotive or your group has found something really difficult to grapple with, some time in quiet together, coming before God, might be a better way to end your time with one another. There are ideas for both kinds of activities below.

WAYS OF PRAYING

STICKY-NOTE PRAYERS

One of the benefits of sticky notes is that they're small. Faced with a whole sheet of A4 paper and being invited to write some prayers could be rather intimidating, but knowing you just need to think of a few words to fill one of those little yellow squares is far less so. Plus the bonus is that you can add a layer of response to the prayers by inviting the members of your group to stick their prayers to something when they've finished. You could even have something available each week to add your prayers to – a cross perhaps, so you can all see the accumulation of your prayers throughout your time together. Alternatively you could have a picture or an artefact each week that ties in with your theme and stick your prayers to that.

EXTEMPORARY PRAYER

Lots of churches will be used to this style of prayer – where you sit together as a group and simply say out loud the words that come to mind. If it's not something your group is used to, occasionally urging them to have a go can be a real encouragement to their faith. Remember that you'll be asking them to publicly declare their faith at the confirmation service, and so praying out loud in their group might be a nice first step.

COLOURING IN

Bear with me – colouring in really is a great way to put your 'wordy' prayers into some kind of creative space. I've printed out black and white versions of beautiful South American crosses before and encouraged groups to colour them in, or brought pads of those geometric designs people can use to colour in. Alternatively you could create illuminated text or letters and begin prayers with these.

COLLAGE

A form of prayer I regularly use in all-age settings is collage prayer. We gather newspapers and cut out images and stories that catch our attention, looking for things that make us want to say thank you; things that trigger within us the desire to ask for God's help; things that make us want to say sorry. We then create collages of those three different headings.

THE JESUS PRAYER

Another ancient form of prayer is the Jesus Prayer. Sometimes we might really struggle to think of the words to say in a given situation; on the other hand, you might have the kind of group who use tons of words but don't actually say anything. The simple words of the Jesus Prayer repeated over and over can help your group slow down and focus on God. They are:

Lord Jesus Christ, Son of God,
have mercy on me a sinner.

You could play some music or just sit quietly, encouraging your group to repeat the words together and maybe building up the time you spend on this over the weeks you're together.

BEADS

Another traditional prayer tool your group might engage with is the making of prayer rosaries. It's a good combination of creativity as well as a helpful aide to prayer. Simply supply the resources to make strings of beads, which the group can create together. You might want to offer each young person the chance to make a string of 20 beads: nine smaller beads for the Jesus Prayer; a larger bead for the grace; nine more for the Jesus Prayer again and then a final larger bead for the Lord's Prayer. (I made a string of 100 beads for this same pattern of prayer while I was at Soul Survivor a decade or more ago and I still use it from time to time.) Encourage your group to be as creative as they like, and maybe add to your creations or change them over the following weeks as your patterns and practices change and evolve.

FOLDED PAPER IN WATER PRAYERS

I'm not sure where this prayer idea originated, but I discovered it in Jenny Baker's book *Heart Soul Mind Strength*.[5] Simply take squares of paper and write thoughts or prayers in the centre. Then fold the corners of each square into the centre to make smaller squares. If you then float the squares, with the flaps uppermost, they'll slowly open out, revealing the prayers inside. It's a really creative way of offering the things on our hearts to God (see Figure 1).

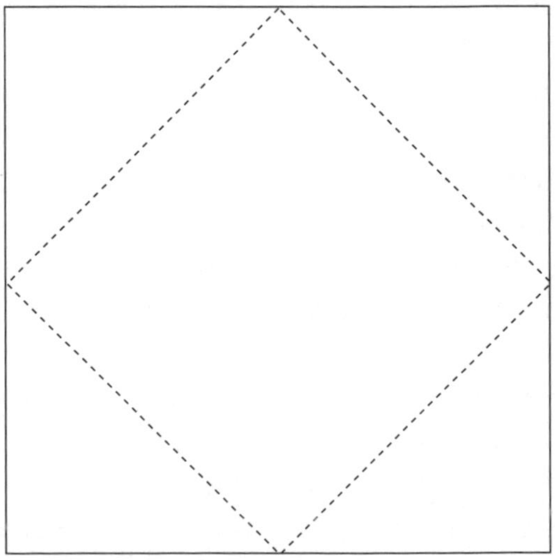

Figure 1 Folded paper in water prayers

ORIGAMI PRAYERS

Another youth worker once introduced me to the idea of paper-crane prayers. The idea is that you hold someone in your heart or your mind as you fold the paper crane – thinking about them, their needs and how you hope God might bless them. It's a good way of slowing down and holding someone before the Lord – with the added bonus of having something to give the person as a sign that you've been praying for them! Just Google 'paper-crane instructions' if you need help.

All of the above activities are things you can do together. They have the added benefit of being things the group can take away and continue in their own time. Some of them might seem a little odd, and there's every chance some in your group might sneer at one or two of them. But it's good to persevere, try things out, reject what doesn't work and expect to be surprised by what does. I wish I'd been offered more ways of engaging with God as a young person, rather than waiting until my mid twenties to find out there were so many ways I could come into his presence.

CLOSING

It seems important somehow for the session to end well, to have a definite moment when you say the meeting is finished and it's time to go. You might want to read a simple blessing to finish each week or say the grace together. If you lit a candle at the start then this would be a good moment to blow it out.

There is a general blessing below, as well as the words of the grace, and a more specific final prayer at the end of each session – feel free to choose whichever suits your group best.

THE GRACE

May the grace of our Lord Jesus Christ,
the love of God, and the fellowship of the
Holy Spirit be with you all.
(2 Corinthians 13.13 NLT)

Amen.

A BLESSING

The LORD bless you
and keep you;
the LORD make his face shine on you
and be gracious to you;
the LORD turn his face towards you
and give you peace.
(Numbers 6.24–26 NIV)

Amen.

PART 2
THE SESSIONS

SECTION 1: THE COMMISSION

1. THE APOSTLES' TEACHING

INTRODUCTION

Reading the Bible is a central element of being a disciple. The Bible is where we hear God's voice on just about every issue that we'll face on our journey. It's the main place where we get to hear God's word to us and it's the source we return to when we want to question teaching, prophecy or revelation. This session will help your group get an idea of the importance of Scripture, discover what Scripture says about itself and discover ways of reading the Bible for themselves.

LEARNING OUTCOMES

By the end of this session your group will have:

- read a passage of Scripture;
- had the opportunity to talk about how they feel about reading the Bible;
- been challenged to get stuck in and read it for themselves.

OPENING WORSHIP

Use one of the ideas from pages 21–2 or the idea below.

In many churches the importance of Scripture is illustrated by the way the Bible is presented to the congregation. Some traditions will have the Bible carried up to the front of church, held aloft so that everyone can see it. The congregation will stand as a mark of respect and the person carrying the Bible will be flanked by people carrying candles. The Bible may even be preceded by someone carrying a thurifer burning incense.

While you might not want to do a full procession with the Bible, you might want to hold it in the air before you walk to wherever you want to stand for the opening words. It would be good to do this without first explaining it to the group – catch them unawares. Mystery or surprise is a good way to start discussion.

Proceed with the candle worship from page 22.

BUSY HANDS

Use one of the activities from page 23 or the idea below.

Journals – you may want to encourage the group to keep journals for the time you spend together preparing for confirmation. If so this would be a good way to get that rolling. Buy enough plain hardbacked notebooks for each member of your group to have one. Have available magazines, old wrapping paper, newspapers and catalogues they can cut up. Try and choose things that will engage your group. While you discuss the questions below, use scissors, pens, glue, sticky tape and sticky-back plastic to decorate and personalize the notebooks. If you want some inspiration, do an online image search for 'decoupage' and see what can be done.

QUESTIONS TO TALK OVER

- What's your favourite book ever? (Why?)
- What's different about reading a story compared to seeing it in a film or on TV?
- How does reading a great book make you feel?

THE BIBLE BIT

A VERSE

I have hidden your word in my heart
that I might not sin against you.
(Psalm 119.11 NIV)

A PASSAGE

Psalm 119.1–16

A LONGER READING

Psalm 119.1–176

QUESTIONS

- What caught your attention from those words? (Why?)
- What do you think God might be trying to get us to notice?
- Why do Christians put such a high emphasis on reading the Bible?
- Do you find the Bible easy or difficult to read? (Why?)
- What could we do to help each other read the Bible more often or to get more from it?

Throughout these questions be aware of what your group is saying and be ready to be honest with your own answers. Lots of young people – and adults – feel very guilty about the regularity with which they read the Bible, so be careful no one feels condemned. Instead make sure that everyone feels encouraged to read the Bible at their own pace and in their own time. The idea of something like the Lectio Divina method of Bible reading is to help people realize how much they can get out of just a few words.

If your group is looking for ways to read the Bible more often, suggest reading notes that they might find helpful or see if you can work together to use social media to help each other along and keep each other accountable. Group members who go to school together might even want to consider ways they can read with each other during school hours – scary but possible!

Also bear in mind that while lots of the young people at confirmation classes will be looking for ways to go deeper with the Bible, for some the Bible might be, quite literally, a closed book. We need to accept that, like many adults, young people's biblical literacy is often very low. If that's the case with your group, start this section with a discussion about what the Bible is and what it's actually for. Do they realize that:

- the Bible is made up of dozens of books written by dozens of people over hundreds of years;
- it's split into two sections: the Old Testament, written before the birth of Christ, and the New Testament, which contains stories about Jesus and the early Church;
- that we share the first five books of the Old Testament with Jews and Muslims, although they call it the Torah or the Tawrat respectively;
- the Bible is made up of all different sorts of writing: history, law, songs/poems and stories?

You may want to spend some time with them unpacking some of these ideas and seeing what myths/misconceptions they have about the Bible. If you want, rather than using the Psalm 119 activity you could read 2 Timothy 3.16–17 together and ask them what they think this tells us about the Bible.

NOTICING GOD

Use one of the ideas from pages 25–6 or the idea below.

HABITS

Ask the group if they have any habits – things they do every day. Make a list.

Ask the group to highlight the things that are a good use of time and those that are a waste of time. Explain that wasting time certainly isn't a negative thing – stopping and resting or just slowing down are things we often lack in contemporary culture.

Suggest to the group that they could each identify one thing they do in their day that's a waste of time – see if anyone fancies taking up the challenge to 'notice God' in a passage of Scripture in these times. For instance: if someone in the group identifies watching TV as a waste of time, suggest that they could read a section of Psalm 119 each day before putting the telly on.

Use it as a challenge for a week and report back at the start of the next session.

CLOSING

Use your regular closing prayer or the following words if you prefer:

Jesus said, 'If you hold to my teaching, you are really my disciples. Then you will know the truth, and the truth will set you free.'
(John 8.31–32 NIV)

Dear Lord, help us to hold to your teachings, to follow your way. Help us to know truth and to discover the freedom that you offer.

Amen.

2. FELLOWSHIP

INTRODUCTION

Getting young people to go to church, and to love it, can be a real challenge. I spend lots of time visiting people in churches who are beside themselves trying to work out what to do with young people when they hit the age of 11 and either slip quietly out of the congregation or leave in spectacular style. There are plenty of young Christian adults who still hold a passion for Christ or an affection for God, but who simply 'don't get' church and will search for any alternative to a Sunday morning in the pew (there's nothing autobiographical about this you understand!). At their confirmation your young people will promise to 'continue in . . . fellowship'.[1] I think this is a very nicely worded bit of liturgy because it doesn't say 'continue going to church'. It's far more subtle than that and maybe even a little subversive.

LEARNING OUTCOMES

By the end of this session your group will have:

- thought about what the early Church looked like;
- considered what they find important about their Christian community;
- thought about how to help each other 'continue in fellowship'.

OPENING WORSHIP

Use one of the ideas from pages 21–2 or the idea below.

There is a well-used picture of the strength of fellowship that describes how burning coals only stay hot when they're in contact with other coals. Remove one coal from the fire and it quickly loses its heat, goes dark and fades, while the coals that remain together keep burning brightly, giving off that wonderful warmth you only get from an open fire.

If you have the wherewithal – and the relevant health and safety measures in place – you could light a fire before the group gathers for your session, either an open fire if you're meeting in a room that has one, or a BBQ or brazier if you have an outdoor space available to you. Start the session by gathering around the fire, see if the conversation naturally turns to the fire and if attention is drawn to it – an open fire will often attract the attention of a group. If the fire doesn't naturally become the focus of attention, you might want to say something simple like 'Let's just watch the flames for a while in quiet.'

After a moment of quiet, take some fire tongs and remove one of the coals or charcoal briquettes from the fire, placing it to one side or on the hearth. You'll notice how quickly it goes dark and loses its heat.

Read these words from Hebrews 10.24–25: 'And let us consider how to provoke one another to love and good deeds, not neglecting to meet together, as is the habit of some, but encouraging one another, and all the more as you see the Day approaching.'

Needless to say this activity requires a certain level of risk assessment. Make sure your group are sensible near the fire, and that you've taken the relevant precautions to make this a safe activity.

BUSY HANDS

Use one of the activities from page 23 or the idea below.

Have a selection of celebrity magazines to hand as well as some blank paper, pens and glue. Also have small pieces of card available big enough to use as place markers at a dinner table.

Ask the group who they'd invite to a party if they could choose anyone from history or the present day. Use the magazines to create a party list and make place names for each of the guests.

QUESTIONS TO TALK OVER

- If you could invite anyone from history to a party, who would you choose? (Why?)
- Do you prefer spending time alone or with a group? (Why?)
- Do you like church?

THE BIBLE BIT

TWO VERSES

Day by day, as they spent much time together in the temple, they broke bread at home and ate their food with glad and generous hearts, praising God and having the goodwill of all the people. And day by day the Lord added to their number those who were being saved.
(Acts 2.46–47)

A PASSAGE

Acts 2.42–47

A LONGER READING

Acts 2.1–47

QUESTIONS

- What caught your attention from these words? (Why?)
- What do you think God might be trying to get us to notice?
- What do you find attractive about this picture of fellowship?
- Does anything worry you or make you feel uneasy about the Acts 2 image of church?
- If we could start from scratch with church, with that Acts 2 picture in mind, what would we create?

If you're the vicar leading this conversation then it might get a little uncomfortable. I can remember very clearly a conversation with a member of the clergy as I gave him feedback from some of the young people about their experience of church. Not surprisingly it was an awkward conversation, with a lot of defensive responses. You need to make sure the group feel they can speak honestly about what they value and appreciate about church, but also the things they struggle with. Resist the urge to defend church or your fellowship, but instead listen carefully to their reflections.

Remember throughout this conversation that the majority of those who make up our present church congregations will be dead in 20 years' time (the Archdeacon of Bournemouth assures me this is an accurate stat), which means that what this group thinks today will *be* the Church in 15–25 years' time.[2]

NOTICING GOD

Use one of the ideas from pages 25–6 or the idea below.

Using paper and pens, cut out a small chain of paper people – there are great instructions at www.wikihow.com/Make-a-Paper-People-Chain. You'll need enough folds to make one person per member of your group, including you as leaders. Get each member to make a chain and then to write their name on everyone else's chain, so that everyone ends up with a chain with everyone's names on it. Encourage them to carry their paper chains around for the week in a pocket, purse or bag, and to thank God for their group every time they see it.

CLOSING

Use your regular closing prayer or the following words if you prefer.

Now on that same day two of them were going to a village called Emmaus, about seven miles from Jerusalem, and talking with each other about all these things that had happened. While they were talking and discussing, Jesus himself came near and went with them. (Luke 24.13–15)

If you had a fire and it's still burning, now would be a good time to toast marshmallows.

3. BREAKING BREAD

INTRODUCTION

Breaking bread together is one of the most defining motifs of the Christian faith. It's one of the few things Jesus specifically told his followers to do and it's something that should bind together Christians of all traditions.

The likelihood is that the young people in your group have sat through hundreds of communion services throughout their lives. Many of them may already take the bread and wine and be a very real part of that community in your church. It's also true that familiarity breeds contempt, and so for some of your group this central activity may have lost some of its significance, simply because of its regularity. For others, of course, confirmation will be the doorway to communion. In our research for *Reconnecting with Confirmation*[1] we discovered that lots of young people were so excited about their confirmation because they could at last take communion. For them this session will serve as a taster of what they have to look forward to – you may want to spend time answering questions about communion. If appropriate to your tradition you could also invite a priest or minister to be part of this session and to lead the **Opening worship**.

LEARNING OUTCOMES

By the end of this session your group will have:

- been reminded of the story of the last supper;
- thought about how they want to be recognized as Christians;
- reflected on Christ's sacrifice for them.

OPENING WORSHIP

Use one of the ideas from pages 21–2 or the idea below.

Conscious of your particular tradition, lay out a table ready for communion. Put a white cloth over the table, smooth it down and make it tidy. Place a plate and a glass on the table. Read these words from the Eucharistic prayer:

Accept our praises, heavenly Father,
through your Son our Saviour Jesus Christ,
and as we follow his example and obey his command,
grant that by the power of your Holy Spirit
these gifts of bread and wine
[hold up the bread and wine]
may be to us his body and his blood;

who, in the same night that he was betrayed,
took bread and gave you thanks;
[pick up and tear in half the bread]
he broke it and gave it to his disciples, saying:
Take, eat; this is my body which is given for you;
do this in remembrance of me.
[pick up the wine and pour some into the glass]

In the same way, after supper
[hold the glass up]
he took the cup and gave you thanks;
he gave it to them, saying:
Drink this, all of you;
this is my blood of the new covenant,

which is shed for you and for many for the
forgiveness of sins.
Do this, as often as you drink it,
in remembrance of me.[2]

Encourage the group to spend a moment in quiet looking at the table with the wine and bread on it, before moving on with the session.

BUSY HANDS

Use one of the activities from page 23 or the idea below.

This will require a certain amount of preparation but will make an ideal activity for you to chat over with your group. Beforehand, gather together all the ingredients to make bread. If you're short of time, have everything weighed out so that the group simply need to mix together pre-prepared ingredients in pairs or by themselves. If you're really short of time, have dough that's been prepared and has gone through its first prove ready for the group simply to knock back and re-knead ready for a second prove and popping in the oven. The internet is full of simple recipes if you don't know how to make bread – see for example www.bbcgoodfood.com/recipes/2060/.

And if baking leavened bread from scratch is going to be too difficult or time consuming you could instead make simple flatbreads or chapattis, which would probably be far closer to the bread Jesus shared with his disciples at the last supper. All you'll need is wholemeal flour, water, a frying pan and a hob (a portable camping stove is perfect for this – I use the little ones with a small gas canister that fits into the side). Simply take 200 g of wholemeal flour and slowly add 75 ml of warm water. Kneed the mixture until you have a good smooth dough. Divide the dough into 6–8 balls and roll them out until they're about the thickness of a 50p piece. Cook the flatbreads over a medium heat for around 30 seconds, then flip them over and cook for about a minute – until they puff up. Remove from the heat and enjoy.

If you're concerned that bread making of any variety is going to be too complicated for your session, focus instead on the cross with your **Busy hands** activity and print out Celtic or South American crosses for your group to colour in as they chat. You can create really special keepsakes if you print out line-drawing versions of South American crosses and then mount them on black card. Colouring in probably wouldn't suit an older group every week but as a one-off they'll probably really enjoy it.

QUESTIONS TO TALK OVER

- What does it feel like to bake your own bread? What do you enjoy most about the process?
- Does baking, or the smell of baking, stir any memories in you – of people or events?
- Do you have anything at home that reminds you of Jesus? What does the cross mean to you?

THE BIBLE BIT

A VERSE

When he was at the table with them, he took bread, blessed and broke it, and gave it to them. Then their eyes were opened, and they recognized him; and he vanished from their sight. *(Luke 24.30–31)*

A PASSAGE

Luke 22.14–20

A LONGER READING

Luke 22.1–71

QUESTIONS

- What caught your attention from these words? (Why?)
- What do you think God might be trying to get us to notice?
- What kinds of emotions do you think the disciples felt as they listened to Jesus' words?
- How do you feel when you take the bread and wine? *or* How do you feel about the prospect of taking the bread and wine?
- Jesus' friends recognized him by the way he broke the bread. How would we be recognized as a friend of Jesus?
- Jesus said that the bread and wine should act as a reminder that his body was broken and his blood poured out. Why do you think he had to/chose to die on the cross?

Obviously some of these questions will need tweaking, depending on whether the members of your group have already been admitted to communion.

NOTICING GOD

Use one of the ideas from pages 25–6 or the idea below.

Introduce this section of the session by watching together a depiction of the crucifixion on video. One of the most compelling, for me, is from the animated movie *The Miracle Maker*,[3] but you may have a favourite you'd like to share with your group.

It's telling that Jesus uses something as simple and commonplace as bread as the thing his disciples are to remember him by. We can find God in the simplest of places and in the simplest of things. Explain to your group that when soldiers go off to war it's traditional for their families to tie a yellow ribbon around a tree as a sign that their relative won't be forgotten while he or she is away. Today we're encouraged to wear coloured ribbons or wristbands to remind us of all sorts of different causes.

Give everyone in your group a short length of purple ribbon and explain that you're going to read some closing words and that you hope they'll take their ribbon and tie it somewhere they'll see it every day. Suggest they might like to use it to remind themselves of the sacrifice Christ made for them, and that each time they see it they might just want to say thank you to him for what he has done.

CLOSING

Read the words of Jesus below and, if your tradition permits it and the young people are happy, share the bread and the wine.

My command is this: love each other as I have loved you. Greater love has no one than this: to lay down one's life for one's friends.
(John 15.12–13 NIV)

4. PRAYER

INTRODUCTION

Alongside reading the Bible, prayer is another cornerstone of Christian discipleship. Communication is vital to any relationship, and communicating with God is the way we best build our friendship with God and explore his heart and what he might be saying to us.

The trouble is that I think we often limit prayer, and in so doing cause issues for our young people. Somehow or other the message seems to be that while there are lots of ways to pray, the best is the hands-together-eyes-closed-talking-in-hushed-tones kind (forgive my stereotyping). Somehow I think we need to help young people realize that while this 'conversing with God' style of prayer using words is a key, it isn't the only or 'best' way. So often young people look at how spirituality is modelled by those at the front in church or at youth events and festivals, and feel that it's an unachievable goal – guilt and disappointment set in.

In this session you'll need to be really honest about your prayer life.

- How does it feel to speak to a God you can't see and often can't hear?
- How do you battle with time and other pressures that try to squeeze out your prayer time (if you have one!)?
- How do other people in the church cope?

LEARNING OUTCOMES

By the end of this session your group will have:

- talked about how they feel about prayer;
- read something about what the Bible has to say about praying;
- spent time in prayer and explored ways to pray.

OPENING WORSHIP

Use one of the ideas from pages 21–2 or the idea below.

SILENT GRACE

In order to overcome the idea of words being all important, try an opening prayer without any words. A silent grace would be one way to do it. Without any introduction, mime the grace, repeat it and see if you can get the group to imitate you – without talking to them. When you've done, and everyone who wants to has had a go, ask: 'Do prayers without spoken words count as real prayers?' 'Why?' 'Why not?'

BUSY HANDS

Use one of the activities from page 23 or the idea below.

Before you begin the questions, invite those who have mobile phones to stack them together, on a table perhaps – you may want to set a forfeit for the first person to take his or her phone from the stack before the end of the session.

QUESTIONS TO TALK OVER

- How does it feel to have your phone out of reach like that?
- Have you ever needed to make a phone call but been unable to because of no signal or a dead battery? What happened? How did it feel?
- Why do we feel the need to communicate with people so strongly?

FONTS

Have a selection of pens (of different thicknesses and colours) and media available, as well as different kinds of paper (coloured, plain, lined, squared and so on).

Invite the group to write out Ephesians 6.18 but in different fonts, inventing their own style (this wording is NIV but use whichever you're happiest with):

> *And pray in the Spirit on all occasions with all kinds of prayers and requests. With this in mind, be alert and always keep on praying for all the Lord's people.*

Encourage them to find a font that looks busy, that looks peaceful, that looks purposeful or relaxed, that communicates efficiency or joy. Encourage them to write in quiet if at all possible. After a while, and before fidgeting sets in, pray for the group, giving thanks to God that he hears us whatever frame of mind we're in and that he loves to hear from us, no matter how we communicate.

THE BIBLE BIT

A VERSE

> *So I say to you: Ask and it will be given to you; seek and you will find; knock and the door will be opened to you.* *(Luke 11.9 NIV)*

A PASSAGE

Luke 11.5–13 (if your group are unfamiliar with the text you'll need to explain that Jesus is answering the request from his disciples to teach them how to pray).

A LONGER READING

Luke 11.1–13

QUESTIONS

- What caught your attention from those words? (Why?)
- What do you think God might be trying to get us to notice?
- Presumably the disciples were devout men. Why do you think they needed Jesus to teach them how to pray?
- When did you last pray? Can you remember what you prayed about?
- If prayer is about more than just talking, what else could we do to communicate with God?

NOTICING GOD

Use one of the ideas from pages 25–6 or the idea below.

Go through a few newspapers and choose some provocative pictures. Some should be positive, others harder to understand. Stick the pictures individually on large sheets of paper, so if you have four pictures you should have four sheets. Have pens, pencils, paint, Play-Doh®, Lego® and so on available for your group.

Invite them to spend a few moments looking at the pictures and considering how they make them feel. Then ask them to choose one and draw, paint or doodle their response to it – without using any words. If possible invite them to do the activity in quiet – put some music on if you think that might help. In my experience we find it very difficult to communicate without words or symbols representing words, so you may need to remind your group that that's the aim of the activity.

After a while ask the group whether these prayers without words are any less prayer than normal 'spoken' prayer. Ask them to explain their answers.

In *Living Your Confirmation* we suggested that young people might like to engage with Anglican Daily Prayer by visiting the Church of England website or getting hold of a copy of *Common Worship*.[1] Since then, the Church has produced a free app for iOS and Android – just search for 'Daily Prayer' in the App Store or in Google Play. Encourage your group that liturgical prayer is an amazing way to join with thousands of other Christians each day, spending time with God.

CLOSING

Use your regular closing prayer or the following words if you prefer:

Very early in the morning, while it was still dark, Jesus got up, left the house and went off to a solitary place, where he prayed. (Mark 1.35 NIV)

Dear Lord, we pray that you help us find the space to spend time with you. Show us how to pray at all times, with or without words.

Amen.

5. RESISTING EVIL

INTRODUCTION

Evil is a funny concept. It's tempting to think that it's an outdated word that we shouldn't really use any more. Journalists on the radio tend to tie themselves up in all sorts of knots trying to avoid labelling someone or something as 'evil'. In some ways that's probably a good thing – we live in a largely liberal society that seeks to find the good in all things and in all people. But we as Christians have to accept the existence of evil and, as a taboo subject, that can be a difficult thing to work through with young people. In their song 'Roll Away your Stone' the band Mumford and Sons sing 'Darkness is a harsh term don't you think? And yet it dominates the things I seek.' To talk about darkness or evil is harsh, but it doesn't take much introspection to discover that there's a darkness that waits to corrupt even our finest intentions.

The point of this session certainly isn't to scare the group, but it also mustn't coddle them. While we're called to recognize and resist evil, the punchline is that God is so much bigger and so much stronger than anything the enemy can throw at us. We know, without a doubt, that God will be victorious!

LEARNING OUTCOMES

By the end of this session your group will have:

- considered the difference between 'scary stuff' and evil;
- talked about the existence of the devil;
- seen how other Christians have stood up to evil.

OPENING WORSHIP

Use one of the ideas from pages 21–2 or the idea below.

You'll need: a spinning top! Have either one you can spin up for the group or a few so they can all have a go.

Spin the top and encourage the group to keep watching it until it stops spinning, either because it hits something, falls off the table or just runs out of momentum. Ask the group why it is that the top doesn't keep spinning forever – they'll come up with all sorts of answers. Explain that in today's session we're going to be thinking about evil – it's the thing that stops us from living for God; the thing that stops us from spinning.

BUSY HANDS

Use one of the activities from page 23 or the idea below.

Print out pictures of a selection of 'baddies' from various different movies and TV shows, include people like Lord Business from *The Lego Movie*, Voldemort from the Harry Potter series, Agent Smith from *The Matrix*, Darth Vader from *Star Wars* and so on. Invite the group to rate them in order of 'evilness' – if it helps, try asking the question 'Who'd win in a fight between . . .?'

QUESTIONS TO TALK OVER

- Have you ever been really scared by something on TV or in a film? (Tread a bit carefully here – try and keep the conversation at *Dr Who* levels rather than *Night of the Living Dead*!)
- Have you ever done anything in real life that you've found frightening?
- What's the difference between something being scary and something being evil?

THE BIBLE BIT

A VERSE

Then Jesus was led by the Spirit into the wilderness to be tempted by the devil. (Matthew 4.1 NIV)

A PASSAGE

Matthew 4.1–11

A LONGER READING

Matthew 3.13—4.11

QUESTIONS

- What caught your attention from these words? (Why?)
- What do you think God might be trying to get us to notice?
- Can you relate to any of Jesus' temptations?
- What do you do when you're tempted to do wrong?
- How do you react to the thought that there might be evil at work in the world (or even in your life)?

NOTICING GOD

Use one of the ideas from pages 25–6 or the idea below.

Divide your group into three and give one of the three stories below to each of these subgroups. Encourage them to read them for themselves. After everyone has had a chance to get acquainted with their story, invite each subgroup to retell what they've read for the benefit of the whole group. (If you only have two or three people in your whole group, either pick one story for all to read together or let them work individually on one each.)

DAVID WILKERSON

Can you imagine selling your TV and devoting the time you spent in front of it in prayer instead? That's what David Wilkerson, a 27-year-old American, did in 1958. One night he decided that instead of spending his evenings watching TV he would commit to pray from midnight to 2 a.m. every night.

Having sold his TV, and while praying, he found himself drawn to a copy of *Time* magazine. At first he thought he must just be suffering from the usual kinds of distractions any one of us struggles with when we set time aside to pray. He turned the distraction over to the Lord and simply asked: 'God, is there something you want me to see?' He recalls the story:

At first glance, it seemed that there was nothing on the page to interest me. It carried a pen drawing of a trial taking place in New York City, 350 miles away. I'd never been to New York, and I never wanted to go, except perhaps to see the Statue of Liberty.

I started to flip the page over. But as I did, my attention was caught by the eyes of one of the figures in the drawing. A boy. One of seven boys on trial for murder. The artist had caught such a look of bewilderment and hatred and despair in his features that I opened the magazine wide again to get a closer look. And as I did, I began to cry.

'What's the matter with me!' I said aloud, impatiently brushing away a tear. I looked at the picture more carefully. The boys were teenagers. They were members of a gang called the Dragons. Beneath their picture was the story of how they had gone into Highbridge Park in New York and brutally attacked and killed a fifteen-year-old polio victim named Michael Farmer. The seven boys stabbed Michael in the back seven times with their knives, then beat him over the head with garrison belts. They went away wiping blood through their hair, saying, 'We messed him good.'

The story revolted me. It turned my stomach. In our little mountain town such things seemed mercifully unbelievable.

That's why I was dumbfounded by a thought that sprang suddenly into my head – full-blown, as though it had come into me from somewhere else: Go to New York City and help those boys.

David Wilkerson was the most unlikely person you could imagine to give up everything and head into New York to work with drug addicts and criminals, but that's exactly what he did – trusted in God, trusted in his calling, and started one of the most famous and well-documented missionary works in the world. Teen Challenge, the charity David Wilkerson eventually started, runs to this day, helping people face life-controlling addiction problems through a Christian faith-based solution.[1]

JACKIE PULLINGER

At the age of 21 Jackie Pullinger stepped off a boat in Hong Kong ready to be a missionary. She had no idea where she should go and no idea what God was calling her to do, just a feeling that this was the right place for her to be. So with just HK$100 in her pocket she found a job as a primary-school teacher in Kowloon, a huge poverty-ridden walled city.

Kowloon was a slum city with little law and no order, ruled instead by the Triad gangs who sold drugs and ran gambling and prostitution rackets across the city.

Jackie was quickly overwhelmed by the desire to help the young people there (many of whom were heavily addicted to drugs), so she began a youth club in an effort to meet with young people, build relationships with them and above all pray with them that they would be released from their drug addictions. Jackie remembers that drug use was so widespread and commonplace that just walking down the street entailed stepping over a hundred people 'chasing the dragon' – smoking their drugs.

One night Jackie arrived at her youth club to discover that it had been so badly vandalized it seemed impossible her ministry could continue. That night she met Winson, an opium addict who'd been sent to 'guard' her. It was when Winson later turned to Christ and was instantly and painlessly freed from his addiction, without any withdrawal symptoms, that Jackie's calling was confirmed: to meet with and pray for healing from drug addiction for the inhabitants of the Walled City of Kowloon.

As she demonstrated her commitment to the city, staying despite having little or no money and despite the disbelief and scepticism of the inhabitants, she slowly began to work an incredible change in that terrifying place.

One by one the boys in her youth club, many of whom had already fallen in with the Triad gangs, turned their lives over to Christ, and as they did so, through prayer, began to be released of their addiction to opium and heroin.

Eventually, in the 1990s, the Walled City was pulled down by the Hong Kong authorities. In its place now stands a park with a model replica of the city and a plaque commemorating the work Jackie did with drug addicts and gang members. Through her charity, St Stephen's Society, her work with drug addicts and the homeless across Asia continues today.[2]

WILLIAM WILBERFORCE

William Wilberforce was a young schoolboy when his fight against evil first began. Before his tenth birthday he wrote his first letter to a newspaper, protesting against slavery.

An incredibly eloquent and intelligent young man, he spent many years exploring what it meant to be a Christian, meeting teachers who told him about a living faith in Jesus and at times battling with his mother, who was concerned about the faith that was growing in him.

At the age of 21 William became an MP and forged strong relationships with other reforming politicians like himself. At 24 he once again came face to face with the Christian faith – and made a commitment to Christ that would change his life forever. His conviction about the evils of the slave trade, combined with his new-found fervour for Jesus Christ and the Bible, combined to form a force that was unstoppable.

Following in the footsteps of others who'd already picked up the batten with regards to the fight against slavery, and horrified by the appalling way slaves were packed into ships like sardines and sailed hundreds of miles around the world, their captors not caring whether they lived or died, Wilberforce committed himself to driving a bill through Parliament abolishing the slave trade once and for all.

In 1789 William delivered a stunning speech in Parliament, forcefully calling for the end to the slave trade, but despite being one of the 'ablest and most eloquent speeches'[3] Parliament had ever heard, and despite being backed by a nationwide campaign, such was the strength of support for slavery in Parliament that the plans were stalled.

Two years later Wilberforce again brought the issue to Parliament. This time it passed, but only after the word 'gradually' was added to the text of the final bill, rendering the decision pointless.

To Wilberforce's great credit he never gave up, in spite of these continual setbacks. By 1805 he'd brought the bill to Parliament no fewer than 11 times and every time he'd been defeated.

It wasn't until 1807, some 18 years after his first speech in Parliament, that eventually slavery was abolished in Great Britain. As Parliament cheered his success, William Wilberforce sat in tears, unable to believe that he'd eventually succeeded in his life's ambition.

You may feel that the stories speak for themselves. If not feel free to use these questions to help the group unpack what they've heard:

- What was the evil in each of the stories?
- How did Christians respond to what they saw?
- What kinds of things can we do as a group to resist evil?

CLOSING

Use your regular closing prayer or the following words from the baptism service if you prefer.

Do not be ashamed to confess the faith of Christ crucified.
Fight valiantly as a disciple of Christ against sin, the world and the devil,
and remain faithful to Christ to the end of your life.

May almighty God deliver you from the powers of darkness,
restore in you the image of his glory,
and lead you in the light and obedience of Christ.[4]

6. REPENT AND RETURN

INTRODUCTION

The likelihood is that you'll have in your group young people with two quite different views on sin. Some of them will be painfully and overly aware of their shortcomings – they'll be able to list all the reasons why they aren't any good, and they'll know full well all their shortcomings. The other group are the ones who have no concept that there's anything wrong in their lives at all – they'll be in love with God (we hope), and so convinced of his love for them that they won't be aware of any need for repentance in their lives. Both positions represent extremes and both are pretty unhealthy for our spiritual well-being.

Being a Christian, is about having an understanding of the shortcomings in our lives but also an understanding of God's love and his grace. I've always loved the idea that when I come to God and tell him I'm not good enough to serve him, he simply replies 'I know – that's the point!'

In this session we don't want to focus entirely on our shortcomings, nor entirely on God's grace. Instead we want to find the balance between acknowledging that we fail and knowing that God sees our failures and forgives us when we come back to him. To use an analogy from *Living Your Confirmation*, we need to identify where the rust patches are in our lives, cut them out and replace them with new, strong metal.[1]

LEARNING OUTCOMES

By the end of this session your group will have:

- gained an understanding of why repentance is important;
- discovered what it means to be absolved of their sins;
- explored some ways of keeping accountable.

OPENING WORSHIP

Use one of the ideas from pages 21–2 or the idea below.

This is a really simple **Opening worship** activity but one that will remind the group of baptism and its role in helping us come before God to repent, be forgiven and mark a new start. You may want to remind the group that in confirmation they're remembering the promises that either they said for themselves at baptism or were said for them if they were baptized as infants. If any of your group are going to be baptized and confirmed at the same service, point out for them what their baptism means.

Simply have two or three bowls of warm water for your group to wash their hands in. You might want to get hold of some really nice soap – the sort they have in posh hotels and restaurants – and some nice clean fluffy towels. As the group wash their hands, and the smell of the soap fills the air, read the following:

Draw near to God, and he will draw near to you. Cleanse your hands, you sinners, and purify your hearts, you double-minded. Lament and mourn and weep. Let your laughter be turned into mourning and your joy into dejection. Humble yourselves before the Lord, and he will exalt you. (James 4.8–10)

BUSY HANDS

Use one of the activities from page 23 or the idea below.

CLEAN IT UP!

Explain to your group that repentance is basically getting cleaned up.

As you explore these opening questions, why not do some cleaning. With permission, get hold of the church silver and some silver cleaning stuff and give it all a good polish – making sure to draw attention to the colour of the rags and the difference in the silver. If you really wanted to make the point you could get some grubby silver-plated stuff from an old cupboard – or even a car boot sale – and see if you can get it from black back to gleaming silver.

QUESTIONS TO TALK OVER

- Have you ever done something really wrong and known that you were going to get into trouble? How did it feel?
- Can you think of times in your life when you've had to make a change in your behaviour or your attitude? Perhaps your parents got bad feedback from a teacher and you knew you had to make some changes.
- How does it feel when you've been in trouble and then things are made right again?

SNOWFLAKES

Make paper snowflakes. Simple as that really: using white paper, fold and cut to make beautiful intricate snowflakes – an image used in Psalm 51 for how pure we are when God forgives us. (I'm something of a pedant when it comes to these things: snowflakes must have 6 sides – you can find useful instructions at www.highhopes.com/snowflakes.html.) You could set a prize for the person who creates the most intricate flake.

THE BIBLE BIT

These verses may need a bit of introducing. Explain to the group that David was a famous King of the Hebrews who served God and led many great victories. Explain too that in the New Testament he is described as 'a man after [God's] heart' (Acts 13.22). Go on to explain that despite serving God so well he is also famous for the most horrendous failure of character. He has an affair with Bathsheba, the wife of one of his commanders, and when she falls pregnant, rather than telling the man what he's done, he has him killed so that he can have Bathsheba as his own wife. The prophet Nathan confronts David about his sin and David writes this incredible prayer of repentance.

A VERSE

Purge me with hyssop, and I shall be clean; wash me, and I shall be whiter than snow. (Psalm 51.7)

A PASSAGE

Psalm 51.1–12

A LONGER READING

Psalm 51

QUESTIONS

- What caught your attention from these words? (Why?)
- What do you think God might be trying to get us to notice?
- Do David's words sound heartfelt?
- Do you think they're enough for the sin he's committed?
- Why do you think that, even after getting it so wrong, God describes David as 'a man after my heart, who will carry out all my wishes'?
- Do you feel God forgives you when you say sorry for your shortcomings?

NOTICING GOD

Use one of the ideas from pages 25–6 or the idea below.

Often it can be really hard to accept God's forgiveness – harder even than asking to be forgiven. Sometimes I think I'd like to have 'Forgiven' tattooed across my body so I can never forget what God has done for me. However, sending your group home from confirmation preparation with tattoos may not go down terribly well, so try this activity instead.

STICKING-PLASTER TATTOOS

You'll need some sticking plasters (the smooth ones will be best as you'll be writing on them), some pens (really fine permanent markers would be great, but ballpoint pens will do) and the words of Psalm 51, either printed out or in the Bible.

Ask the group to re-read Psalm 51 and to pick out all the words that suggest forgiveness: 'washed', 'cleansed', 'purged', 'clean', 'new', 'right', 'restored' and 'delivered' are all possibilities.

Ask the group to think which two or three words most catch their attention; to write them on the sticking plasters (as creatively as they like); to stick the plasters on themselves.

CLOSING

Use your regular closing prayer or the following words if you prefer.

If we confess our sins, he who is faithful and just will forgive us our sins and cleanse us from all unrighteousness. (1 John 1.9)

Help us Lord God to be the kind of people who keep a clean slate with you, who are always ready to accept that we have done wrong, to turn round and to follow you again.

Amen.

7. PROCLAIM THE GOOD NEWS

INTRODUCTION

On the surface this seems like a fairly straightforward statement – the promise to 'proclaim the good news'. But the more Christians I talk to the more diverse an understanding of the phrase 'good news' I discover. For many the good news is simply the retelling of the gospel story as relayed in Scripture; for others it's living a life of generosity and kindness as demonstrated by Jesus. For most, of course, it's a combination of the two, even if the emphasis may remain on one or the other. There is a range of theological understandings as to what is important in proclaiming the good news, but for the purposes of this session, and for our young people as they work towards their confirmation, it's a realization that our faith isn't for keeping to ourselves, rather it's for sharing. In this session you'll help your group try to grapple with what they understand the good news to be, so that they know what it is they're promising to proclaim.

LEARNING OUTCOMES

By the end of this session your group will have:

- considered what it is about the Christian message that is 'good news';
- thought about why it's important to proclaim that message;
- thought of ways to encourage each other to share the story.

OPENING WORSHIP

Use one of the ideas from pages 21–2 or the idea below.

Give everyone in your group a glow stick, but tell them not to crack them just yet. You can get glow sticks from big supermarkets or pound shops, and if all else fails they're cheap on eBay. If possible, get the ones that have connectors and can be turned into bracelets/wrist bands.

Read these words from Matthew 5, and break and shake your stick as you read the words 'let your light shine'.

> *You are the light of the world. A town built on a hill cannot be hidden. Neither do people light a lamp and put it under a bowl. Instead they put it on its stand, and it gives light to everyone in the house. In the same way, let your light shine before others, that they may see your good deeds and glorify your Father in heaven.*
>
> *(Matthew 5.14–16 NIV)*

Now wrap the glow sticks around your wrists and continue with the session.

BUSY HANDS

Use one of the activities from page 23 or the idea below.

You'll need either a computer/tablet with an internet connection or a selection of 'inspirational' photos on a computer that's offline. Ask the group to use the computer to make a slide show of photos that will help people discover God – they might think of beautiful landscape pictures, photos of people helping others, children playing or similar. If you're on the internet, searching Flickr or Google Images for example, it might be worth checking that you have parental controls switched on – better safe than sorry! If you have the software then you can use the 'Ken Burns effect' to give the slide show a more professional animated feel, and you could choose some music to play in the background. (For a simple option use the free 'Picasa' software from Google, select the pictures you want to use then click 'create movie' and select the 'pan and zoom' option.)

QUESTIONS TO TALK OVER

- Have you ever had to wait for some news you've been really desperate to hear, such as the birth of a sibling, exam results or similar?
- How does it feel to have to wait for news you're really desperate for?
- How did it feel when you got the news? Was it good or bad? Was it what you expected?

THE BIBLE BIT

TWO VERSES

The Spirit of the Lord is on me,
because he has anointed me
to proclaim good news to the poor.
He has sent me to proclaim freedom for the prisoners
and recovery of sight for the blind,
to set the oppressed free,
to proclaim the year of the Lord's favour.
(Luke 4.18–19 NIV)

A PASSAGE

Luke 4.14–22

A LONGER READING

Luke 4

QUESTIONS

- What caught your attention from these words? (Why?)
- What do you think God might be trying to get us to notice?
- Why do you think we call the message of Jesus 'good news'?
- If someone asked you why you were a Christian, what do you think you'd say?
- Can you think of things you do that are good news to other people?
- What things could you do?

NOTICING GOD

Use one of the ideas from pages 25–6 or the idea below.

PERSON, PEOPLE, PLACE

Group members might want to take this opportunity to think about how they can become proclamation people. Help them to think about proclaiming the good news in its widest sense by getting them to consider how to share it on a number of levels.

This final activity will require a little more preparation than usual. You'll need to get each member of the group to make wool felt balls and then to string them together. The balls are really simple to make and look great when they're done, but because each one takes a few moments to complete, it provides an opportunity for your group to stop and think, and by stringing them together with a little fishing line at the end, they've got something to carry around as a reminder of who they've been thinking about. You can buy carded wool or felting wool cheaply on eBay. For great instructions on how to make the balls, look at this YouTube video: http://youtu.be/H3dlO_1qlHY.

As they make each ball, rolling the wool around with the soap and water, they need to spend a few moments thinking first about a person they feel needs to hear the good news, then a group of people and then a place or situation. You should try to help them think about how the good news might be different depending on whom they're sharing it with, which also reinforces the idea that the gospel isn't just a thing for individuals – it's good news for whole communities. We're called to share the gospel with our neighbour but also to take it to the ends of the earth.

If that all sounds a bit arty-crafty for your group, try making elastic-band balls instead. Simply buy the biggest bag of elastic bands you can find, and have a marble for each young person. Use the marble as the core and then, starting with the smaller elastic bands, wrap them round and round the core until you have as big a ball as possible. If you're confused, there's a YouTube tutorial here: http://youtu.be/bNyHIxqr6SU.

Use this as a way to think about proclaiming the gospel being a many layered thing, from simply the way you treat the people you meet every day right up to stretching yourself and travelling across the globe to engage in overseas mission of some kind.

CLOSING

Use your regular closing prayer or the following words if you prefer:

> I consider my life worth nothing to me; my only aim is to finish the race and complete the task the Lord Jesus has given me – the task of testifying to the good news of God's grace.
> (Acts 20.24 NIV)

If your group made the felt balls, they may want to hold them while they think about these words.

8. SEEK AND SERVE CHRIST IN ALL PEOPLE

INTRODUCTION

The actual phrase from the confirmation service is, 'Will you seek and serve Christ in all people, loving your neighbour as yourself?'[1] I'm acutely conscious that this is a far more theologically complicated statement than simply a command to us to serve other people, which is the subject of this session. If your group are up for it, you may want to spend some time with them reflecting on what it means to seek Christ in all people, especially if they're the kind of group with a very black-and-white, Christian/non-Christian view of the world.

In many of our churches young people are totally at home with serving – it's often the role we assign them. If chairs need moving, tables stacking or food needs serving, we often turn to the youth group. As you explore this topic, consider whether you could be engaging them more regularly in preaching, teaching and leading worship as well as those more simple acts of service. Bear in mind that we're all called to the role of servant before anything else, and that serving isn't something the young should do out of politeness or sense of duty, rather as an expression of gratitude for the love God has shown them.

In *Going for Growth*, the Church of England's 2010 report on work with children and young people, Anne Richards notes that just like adults, young people are called to be 'active citizens in the kingdom of God on earth'.[2] God has created each of them with gifts and abilities, which he expects them to use. No one is a passenger in the kingdom!

LEARNING OUTCOMES

By the end of this session your group will have:

- considered the way Jesus came to serve;
- considered what their gifts are and how they might use them for God's glory;
- reflected on the idea that Christ is in all people.

OPENING WORSHIP

Use one of the ideas from pages 21–2 or the idea below.

FOOT WASHING

Jesus washing his friends' feet was perhaps one of the most powerful symbols of his desire for us to understand the nature of his kingdom. It made very clear that with God the highest position is held by the one most at ease with serving. Jesus, the king of the universe, gets on his hands and knees and washes the muck from his friends' feet. It's an amazing image.

This **Opening worship** will be most effective if you're happy to wash the feet of the members of your group. If that's not something you're comfortable with you can wash their hands or get them to wash each other's hands. It's up to you.

Have bowls of warm water ready and towels. Read these words from John:

Jesus knew that the Father had put all things under his power, and that he had come from God and was returning to God; so he got up from the meal, took off his outer clothing, and wrapped a towel around his waist. After that, he poured water into a basin and began to wash his disciples' feet, drying them with the towel that was wrapped round him . . . When he had finished washing their feet, he put on his clothes and returned to his place. 'Do you understand what I have done for you?' he asked them. 'You call me "Teacher" and "Lord", and rightly so, for that is what I am. Now that I, your Lord and Teacher, have washed your feet, you also should wash one another's feet. I have set you an example that you should do as I have done for you. Very truly I tell you, no servant is greater than his master, nor is a messenger greater than the one who sent him. Now that you know these things, you will be blessed if you do them.'

(John 13.3–5, 12–17 NIV)

BUSY HANDS

Use one of the activities from page 23 or the idea below.

ACTS OF SERVICE

Why not engage in some kind of act of service as you set up the topic this week? Find a small job to do around where you meet, and chat over the questions below as you do it. You could do a litter-pick around the building or pull out some weeds in the grounds. Perhaps you could do some washing up or some other kind of cleaning activity. Maybe there are some envelopes that need stuffing for a church mailing, or newsletters that need folding – you get the idea!

If your group enjoy this small act of service, perhaps they could keep on doing it in the following weeks.

QUESTIONS TO TALK OVER

- How do you feel when someone asks you to do a job?
- Are there any chores that you'd never do?
- How does it feel when you do something that someone is really grateful for?

THE BIBLE BIT

TWO VERSES

Christ was truly God.
But he did not try to remain equal with God.
Instead he gave up everything and became a slave,
when he became like one of us.

(Philippians 2.6–7 CEV)

A PASSAGE

Philippians 2.1–11

A LONGER READING

Philippians 2

QUESTIONS

- What caught your attention from these words? (Why?)
- What do you think God might be trying to get us to notice?
- Why do you think God sent Christ as a servant rather than an all-powerful conquering king?
- In the confirmation service you're going to promise to 'seek and serve Christ in all people'. Is it always easy to see Christ in people? What should we be looking for?
- What kind of attitude do you think God asks of us?
- What gifts do you think God has given you to use in his service?

NOTICING GOD

Use one of the ideas from pages 25–6 or the idea below.

A CHRIST-LIKE PERSON

On a large sheet of paper draw the rough outline of a person. Get the group to list all the things a 'Christ-like person' would look like – think about character as well as appearance.

Once you've got a good list, grab another pen – something big and bold – and write these words over the top of everything that's already been written: 'hungry', 'thirsty', 'naked', 'sick', 'a stranger', 'a prisoner'. Explain that in Matthew 25 Jesus says that whenever we look after people like this we're looking after him. Allow a moment of quiet for the group to reflect and then move into the closing.

CLOSING

Use your regular closing prayer or the following words of Mother Teresa[3] if you prefer:

Make us worthy Lord to serve our fellow
men throughout the world,
who live and die in poverty and hunger.
Give them through our hands, this day, their
daily bread
and by our understanding love give peace
and joy.

Amen.

9. ACKNOWLEDGE CHRIST'S AUTHORITY

INTRODUCTION

Christ was a pretty authoritative figure (there's an understatement!). In *Living your Confirmation*[1] we invite young people to reflect on the ways Christ demonstrates his absolute authority: over people, with his irresistible call to Simon and Andrew to drop their nets (Matthew 4.20); over nature, when he stops a storm in its tracks with a word (Mark 4.35–41); over spirits, when he casts Legion out of the possessed Gerasene man (Mark 5.1–20); over sickness, when he heals the woman who's been bleeding for many years (Mark 5.25–34); and over death when he raises Jairus' daughter (Mark 5.35–43). While it would be good to have time to read all five passages in this session (and so many more besides), it probably isn't practical, so instead we're going to focus on one of the best-known stories of Jesus using his authority to change someone's life dramatically.

The group will probably know the story of Zacchaeus inside out. This session will help them think it through one more time and then to wonder what Christ might ask of them if he were to join them for dinner.

LEARNING OUTCOMES

By the end of this session your group will have:

- reflected on Christ's authority;
- seen the good that can come when someone submits to Christ;
- reconsidered the areas of their lives where they need to submit to him.

OPENING WORSHIP

Use one of the ideas from pages 21–2 or the idea below.

Everything was created by him,
everything in heaven and on earth,
everything seen and unseen,
including all forces and powers,
and all rulers and authorities.
All things were created by God's Son,
and everything was made for him.
God's Son was before all else,
and by him everything is held together.
(Colossians 1.16–17 CEV)

On a large piece of paper draw a big circle and place a candle at the centre of it. Ask one of the group to read the verses above out loud, and as they do so, place things inside the circle to represent what God has authority over – for instance:

- people – a Playmobil® or Lego® figure;
- technology – a mobile phone;
- rulers and authorities – a crown or a picture of a crown;
- nature – an apple.

When the reading is finished, ask the group what else they could put in the circle as symbols of things God has authority over.

BUSY HANDS

Use one of the activities from page 23 or the idea below.

MAKING MONEY

Decorating biscuits may sound like a Sunday School activity but it'll be fun and there'll be something delicious to eat at the end! Have enough round biscuits for everyone to have a couple (rich tea or digestives are probably best), as well as some gloopy icing (mix icing with a little water to make gorgeous, gloopy icing – you can never have too much!). Also have available some writing icing (gold and silver if you can get it) and other sparkly shiny cake decorating stuff. Use all the ingredients to make super-sweet edible coins.

QUESTIONS TO TALK OVER

- Do you get an allowance or pocket money?
- What kinds of things do you spend your money on?
- How generous would you say you are?

THE BIBLE BIT

A VERSE

Zacchaeus stood up and said to the Lord, 'Look, Lord! Here and now I give half of my possessions to the poor, and if I have cheated anybody out of anything, I will pay back four times the amount.' (*Luke 19.8* NIV)

A PASSAGE

Luke 19.1–10

A LONGER READING

Luke 19

QUESTIONS

- What caught your attention from these words? (Why?)
- What do you think God might be trying to get us to notice?
- What do you think it was about Jesus that made Zacchaeus so quick to change his life?
- What do you think life in Jericho might have been like after Jesus had passed through?

NOTICING GOD

Use one of the ideas from pages 25–6 or the idea below.

Here we're going to use a guided reflection to help the group put themselves in Zacchaeus' shoes and consider what meeting Jesus might mean for them. Invite your group to make themselves comfortable, sitting or lying if appropriate, and when it's quiet, start the reading.

Imagine it's hot. Hot and dry, with a wind blowing dust off the desert. The town is busy, busier than normal, with people shouting and singing. Someone has come to town, someone eagerly anticipated, and you're as keen to get your eyes on him as anyone else. You hurry through the streets to where you know the visitor will be making his way through the crowds, but try as you might, you can't get anywhere near the front – sharp elbows and harsh words keep you from pushing forwards. About to give up, you notice a tree a little way ahead that reaches over the road. If you could just get there quick enough and scramble into the branches, you might just get a glimpse of the man who's come to town. Dodging ahead you reach the tree and, with little elegance, haul yourself into its branches, catching your clothes and your skin on the way up. You settle on to a branch and as you do the guest, the focus of all your effort, approaches your refuge. Then, to your horror, rather than passing by, he stops, right under your hiding place. And then, as if it had been his intention all along, maybe the whole reason he stopped in your town, he looks up into the tree and straight into your eyes.

Listen as Jesus speaks your name. How does he say it? How does it make you feel to be recognized and singled out? What races through your mind as he tells everyone that he is coming back to yours for a while? What preparations do you wish you could make? What things do you wish you could hide?

As you look into those dark brown eyes, you recognize the look of complete authority. What might Jesus be asking you to change?

Leave the group in quiet for a short while and then draw them back before they become restless. If appropriate, and if anyone is willing, invite them to share what Jesus said to them.

CLOSING

Finish this session with this prayer:

We pray for our leaders 'and others in power, so that we may live quiet and peaceful lives as we worship and honour God'.
(1 Timothy 2.1–2 CEV)

Amen.

If you started with the candle-in-a-circle activity, you may want to use this moment to encourage the group to write their names inside the circle as a way of showing that they want to live under God's authority.

10. DEFENDING THE WEAK

INTRODUCTION

I'm always struck that when we think of the weak and the poor, our thoughts often turn to the pictures we see on TV of starving people in countries far, far away. For centuries the Church has responded to God's call to defend the weak by travelling to those distant countries and doing mission works. And that makes real sense. I imagine that when you've seen the kind of poverty people suffer in a war-torn, drought-ridden country, the relative poverty we see in this country must look somewhat insubstantial.

The trouble with this view is that it can leave young people thinking that defending the weak and seeking peace and justice is something that can only be done by travelling thousands of miles, or when they have enough money to support the kinds of charities that can do that work on our behalf. The challenge for young people is to help them to recognize the weak in their daily spheres; to look for, and find, signs of injustice in their worlds; to know how to respond.

Here I borrow several ideas from the confirmation follow-up book *Living Your Confirmation*.[1] That book will help your group earth what they discover in this session.

LEARNING OUTCOMES

By the end of this session your group will have:

- considered how Jesus responded to injustice;
- looked for signs of injustice in the wider world and in their day-to-day lives;
- thought of ways to be people who seek peace and justice.

OPENING WORSHIP

Use one of the ideas from pages 21–2 or the idea below.

Have a selection of artefacts ready for the group to gather around. Include:

- a bowl of water;
- a lemon;
- a pound coin;
- a roll of thread with a needle;
- some thick gloves – ski mittens ideally;
- a bowl of dry porridge oats;
- a pile of stones big and heavy enough to hold and feel (preferably the kind of river stones you can get from garden centres).

As they look at the artefacts, read this prayer:

Lord God, today is going to be a difficult session as we think about the injustice that exists in the world you created. As we consider those people who work to make our clothes for next to no money, those who have no access to clean water or a good meal, those who live in fear of violence and pain, help us to hear your voice and know your love.

Amen.

BUSY HANDS

Use one of the activities from page 23 or the idea below.

Using the artefacts from **Opening worship**, get the group to have a go at these tricky challenges.

LEMON BALANCE

Float a lemon in a bowl of water and then invite the group to try to balance the pound coin on it.

THREAD THE NEEDLE

Invite the group to try to thread the needle while wearing the thick gloves.

DRY OATS

Challenge the group to eat a full desert spoon of the oats in less than 30 seconds, with no water – but first check for allergies.

STONE STACK

Try and make the biggest possible stack of the pebbles (like Jenga® but rockier . . .).

QUESTIONS TO TALK OVER

- When was the last time you said, 'It's not fair'? What had happened?
- When you see pictures of refugees or starving children on the TV, how does it make you feel?
- Have you ever done anything to help someone in need? (Encourage the group to think about ways they've actually helped someone out, rather than given money or raised sponsorship.)

THE BIBLE BIT

A VERSE

The Lord God has told us
what is right
and what he demands:
'See that justice is done,
let mercy be your first concern,
and humbly obey your God.'
(Micah 6.8 CEV)

A PASSAGE

John 8.1–11 (If you use this reading, it might be worth reading the version in *Living Your Confirmation*, which has a guided meditation feel that should help the group engage with each of the characters in the text.[2])

A LONGER READING

As this is a self-contained story, I'm not including a longer reading in this session.

QUESTIONS

- What caught your attention from these words? (Why?)
- What do you think God might be trying to get us to notice?
- With which characters in the story did you relate?
- How do you think God distinguishes between the poverty and injustice we see on TV from around the world, and the kinds of poverty people suffer in our country?
- From this story, what about Jesus' character inspires you? How can you be like him in the face of injustice?

NOTICING GOD

Use one of the ideas from pages 25–6 or the idea below.

One of the symbols of poverty is the cardboard box. It's the kind of thing we associate with people who are unable to afford a house and are living rough on the streets, or maybe in less developed nations where people have to build their own house in a shanty town or favela. Before the session, prepare by tearing chunks out of some brown corrugated cardboard, enough for everyone to have a piece and big enough to write the words of Micah 6.8 on them. You might also want to do an online image search of homelessness and shanty towns and have a picture projected on a slide show or printed out for the group to see.

Encourage your group to write the words from Micah 6.8 on their piece of card and to take it home and put it somewhere they can see it. Remind them that when they see poverty they don't need to despair because God will help them to know how to respond.

CLOSING

You'll need some more artefacts for this section: each group member will need a stone (from the pile at the start of the session); a bread roll; a pound coin (feel free to use 10p pieces if your group is big!).

Ask the group to hold the three things they've been given and then read this reflection to them:

- When we see injustice we, as Christians, are compelled to respond.
- As you hold the stone, think of the people who cause injustice – politicians, bullies, maybe yourself. How will you stand up to them?
- As you hold the money, think of the people far away who are living lives of fear and poverty. How can you support the groups and charities working to bring peace and justice?
- As you hold the bread, think of the injustices you see around you each day – the homeless, the outcasts, the poor. What can you do to touch those around you with Christ's love?

SECTION 2: ISSUES

11. SEX

INTRODUCTION

Not surprisingly, this topic needs careful handling – partly because it's a sensitive issue with all sorts of ramifications, but mostly because the way you handle it could have a major effect on the way your group of young people continue in their faith journey. The reason is this: in all likelihood the members of your group are as sexually active as their non-Christian friends. I know youth workers who struggle to believe this, but my strong suspicion is that it's true. Sadly, I'm not aware of any research in the UK that looks at sex and faith, but a 2009 report in the USA was clear that some 80 per cent of unmarried evangelical young adults said they'd had sex – only slightly less than the 88 per cent of unmarried adults without an evangelical faith.[1] I suspect that the UK stats are probably very similar. In *You Lost Me*, David Kinnaman cites traditional church views on sex and sexuality as one of the key reasons why young American Christians leave church. I recommend reading his thoughts as a good preparation for this session.[2]

I think the way we in church have traditionally talked about sex can have very negative outcomes. In young people who are already sexually active I've seen two responses: some will hear that sex should be saved for marriage, reflect that as they've already had sex it's too late for them and so they may as well just get on with it; others will feel so ashamed at what they've done that they'll give up their faith because they feel God could never forgive them. Those who aren't sexually active hear the message that purity is the number-one goal of the Christian faith, and so long as they haven't had sex, everything is all right – it becomes the main point of being a Christian. I've often joked that for many Christian youth workers the main aim of youth ministry seems to be getting a young person to university without them losing their virginity – we somehow think it's the main goal of discipleship!

I'm conscious that as Christian leaders we tread a very difficult line here. On the one hand we need to teach Christian values, and sexual purity is an important part of that; on the other we need to keep a firm hold on grace and forgiveness. We need to get sex into perspective.

For a number of reasons, finding a Bible verse that specifically speaks out against sex before marriage is really difficult. There's plenty of thought about adultery and promiscuity, but when Jewish people from Bible times tended to marry at the age of 13 or so, sex before that age would have been no less taboo than underage sex is now. For some this means that teaching abstinence to young people today, who may not marry until their late twenties or early thirties, makes little sense biblically. For the purpose of this material we're going to stick to the traditional teaching of maintaining sexual purity until marriage, but I encourage you to consider the implications for the members of your group.

Pornography is such a huge issue for young people that I've written about it in a separate chapter (see page 86).

LEARNING OUTCOMES

By the end of this session your group will have:

- explored some of the things the Bible has to say about sex;
- considered the reasons behind some traditional views on sex outside marriage;
- reflected on the balance between purity and grace.

OPENING WORSHIP

You really want a worship activity that 'de-giggles' your group – and calms your own nerves if we're being honest. I suggest you use the centring exercise from page 21 for today's opening worship.

If you're feeling brave and want to set the scene with a Bible verse that demonstrates that sex is a good thing, which God created and approves of, you might want to use these words from the Song of Solomon:

My darling, I am yours, and you desire me.
Let's stroll through the fields
and sleep in the villages.
At dawn let's slip out and see if grapevines
and fruit trees are covered with blossoms.
When we are there, I will give you my love.
(Song of Solomon 7.10–12 CEV)

BUSY HANDS

Use one of the activities from page 23 or the idea below.

Buy a few magazines or Sunday supplements – choose the ones with the most adverts. Go through the magazines and pull out every advert that uses sex – however subtly – to sell something. Make a collage – but probably best not put it up on the church wall . . .

QUESTIONS TO TALK OVER

- Have you ever been in love? What was (is) it like?
- Do you think attitudes to sex have changed since your parents were your age? How? Why?
- How would you describe your church's attitude to sex? Do you think it's got it right?

THE BIBLE BIT

A VERSE

Have respect for marriage. Always be faithful to your partner, because God will punish anyone who is immoral or unfaithful in marriage.
(Hebrews 13.4 CEV)

A PASSAGE

1 Corinthians 7.1–4

A LONGER READING

1 Corinthians 7.1–4 and 1 Thessalonians 4.1–8

QUESTIONS

- What caught your attention from those words? (Why?)
- What do you think God might be trying to get us to notice?
- The Bible doesn't directly contain any teaching on sex before marriage – why do you think that is? (See the notes at the start of this chapter for some thoughts on this.)
- The 1 Corinthians passage speaks positively about sex as a part of marriage. There are plenty of passages that have far stronger things to say about sexual immorality and adultery – why do you think that 1 Corinthians is a good place to start?
- Do you think this is a popular message? Why? Why not?

NOTICING GOD

Use one of the ideas from pages 25–6 or the idea below.

The idea here is to send the young people out looking for God's grace at work, rather than looking at how they might be at risk of 'sexual sin'. I sometimes think we become so obsessed with remaining pure from sexual immorality that by definition we become obsessed with sex, when what would be far healthier would be to direct our attention to God.[3]

You'll need a compass (or two or three depending on the size of your group), some magnets and, if you made it, the collage from the **Busy hands** section above – if not, just a large sheet of blank paper will do, or simply a table top.

Place the compass at the centre of the table and draw the group's attention to the fact that it points to true north. Slowly introduce the magnets around the edge of the sheet and watch what happens to the compass – it gets pulled away from true north of course. Ask the group to consider for a moment what their distractions might be; what pulls their attention away from God. Ask them to name the magnets – either out loud or in their heads – and then to lift the magnets carefully away. As they're removed one by one, what happens to the needle on the compass?

Ask the group to think what things they can use to keep their focus on God. Then ask how they can help each other to keep facing 'true north'.

CLOSING

Use your regular closing prayer or the following words if you prefer:

Surely your goodness and love will follow me
all the days of my life,
and I will dwell in the house of the LORD
for ever. (Psalm 23.6 NIV)

Help us to stay close to you, Lord Jesus,
to keep our eyes on the true north.

Amen.

12. ALCOHOL

INTRODUCTION

It was tempting to write four chapters at this point covering drink, drugs, smoking and other intoxicants, but it quickly became clear that it would be quite difficult to come up with separate material for each. If you're aware of particular issues in your group with smoking or illegal drugs, I suggest you run separate sessions on these outside of confirmation preparation, exploring some of the specific problems that arise. This session is aimed more at thinking about intoxication, and alcohol is how most of our young people will experience that.

The colleague with whom I work most closely came to the diocese from a Baptist and then Scripture Union background. For about the first year working with us, one sentence was repeated over and again: 'There's wine with *everything* in the Anglican Church!' He couldn't believe how much alcohol we Anglicans consume!

It's with these words ringing in my head that I want to introduce this session with a healthy dose of reality. When we were teenagers we – mostly – drank alcohol. I remember very clearly my first experience of getting drunk; it involved lager, a liqueur and a doner kebab. And, yes, I was ill. My second point is that according to research, it's middle-class parents who are among some of the heavier drinkers in the UK,[1] and while we don't make the headlines like young drinkers, there are very real concerns about the amount of alcohol consumed by this group.

My point is simple: young people aren't stupid. They know when we're speaking honestly. My advice in this session is to be honest with your group. Don't tell them the story you think they're meant to hear, rather tell them about your experience and your values.

We know Jesus didn't have an issue with the consumption of alcohol; he drank wine with his friends and he once miraculously created gallons of wine for people who'd already had 'too much to drink' (you'll look at the Wedding at Cana as part of this session). What the Bible seems very clear about is that drunkenness is wrong. This session will be an opportunity for you to explore why people drink alcohol and to think about the difference between responsible and irresponsible drinking.

LEARNING OUTCOMES

By the end of this session your group will have:

- read some of the things the Bible has to say about alcohol;
- considered why people drink and why sometimes they drink to excess;
- explored the difference between drinking and drunkenness.

OPENING WORSHIP

For this opening section of the session you'll need to buy and download a copy of Pip Wilson's *Blob Bar* picture at www.blobtree.com/products/blob-bar. The Blobs, a classic youth-work tool, have been around for years. They help young people – people of all ages really – to engage with subjects in a non-judging, non-sensationalist way. For more information visit www.blobtree.com/pages/frontpage.

Encourage the group to spend some time looking at the Blob picture and to think about which Blob might best represent them individually. Encourage anyone who feels like it to explain why they've chosen a specific Blob. Either print the image out large and all share the same one, or give each of the group their own copy so that they can spend some time thinking it through for themselves.

BUSY HANDS

Use one of the activities from page 23 or the idea below.

It's cocktail time! Well, non-alcoholic cocktails anyway... Have ready a selection of things like fruit juices, chopped fruit, lemonade and ice, as well as cocktail glasses, paper umbrellas and so on. If you can get hold of a couple of cocktail shakers – even better!

Make cocktails! If you want recipes there are loads on the internet – just search for 'non-alcoholic cocktail recipes'. I found a good list here, at www.netmums.com/family-food/party-food/non-alcoholic-cocktails.

QUESTIONS TO TALK OVER

- What is it about drinking alcohol that's so appealing? (Try to get past the 'Because it's cool' answer and into some of the other reasons: it tastes good, it relaxes you, it removes inhibitions and so on.)
- What are some of the downsides to drinking alcohol?
- What do you think your church's stance is on alcohol consumption? Do you agree with it or not?

THE BIBLE BIT

A VERSE

Be alert and of sober mind. Your enemy the devil prowls around like a roaring lion looking for someone to devour. (1 Peter 5.8 NIV)

For this session I recommend reading two passages side by side here (shown on the next page). One is the passage from Proverbs 23 that advises against drinking wine, the other is the story of Jesus turning water into wine at the wedding in Cana.

QUESTIONS

- What caught your attention from these words? (Why?)
- What do you think God might be trying to get us to notice?
- Do these passages contradict each other?
- From these two passages, what can we understand about God's feelings about alcohol?
- Why do you think the Bible warns us against drunkenness?

NOTICING GOD

Use one of the ideas from pages 25–6 or the idea below.

You'll need the Blob picture from the start of the session again. As the group look at it for a second time, ask them why they think the different people in the picture are drinking. Explore some of the common reasons people give – boredom, confidence, to fit in, curiosity and so on.

After a while, and when some of the Blobs have been labelled, ask the group to consider what other things people could do to counter these negative feelings: 'When you're bored, rather than drinking, you could…'

If it helps, run this session in the third person so that the group can talk about hypothetical friends rather than having to talk about themselves. Sometimes this can be easier, particularly if you have someone in your group who's struggling with any of the issues raised.

Finally, with the Bible readings from earlier in mind, ask the group if they can identify any of the Blobs as Jesus, or if not, where would Jesus be in the picture and what would he be doing?

CLOSING

Use your regular closing prayer or the following words if you prefer:

On this mountain the LORD Almighty will prepare a feast of rich food for all peoples, a banquet of aged wine – the best of meats and the finest of wines. (Isaiah 25.6 NIV)

Lord Jesus, we look forward to joining you in your Kingdom for an unimaginable feast. Keep us close to you until that time.

Amen.

Who has woe? Who has sorrow?
Who has strife? Who has complaints?
Who has needless bruises? Who has bloodshot eyes?
Those who linger over wine,
who go to sample bowls of mixed wine.
Do not gaze at wine when it is red,
when it sparkles in the cup,
when it goes down smoothly!
In the end it bites like a snake
and poisons like a viper.
Your eyes will see strange sights,
and your mind will imagine confusing things.
You will be like one sleeping on the high seas,
lying on top of the rigging.
'They hit me,' you will say, 'but I'm not hurt!
They beat me, but I don't feel it!
When will I wake up
so I can find another drink?' (Proverbs 23.29–35 NIV)

On the third day a wedding took place at Cana in Galilee. Jesus' mother was there, and Jesus and his disciples had also been invited to the wedding. When the wine was gone, Jesus' mother said to him, 'They have no more wine.'

'Woman, why do you involve me?' Jesus replied. 'My hour has not yet come.'

His mother said to the servants, 'Do whatever he tells you.'

Nearby stood six stone water jars, the kind used by the Jews for ceremonial washing, each holding from eighty to a hundred and twenty litres.

Jesus said to the servants, 'Fill the jars with water'; so they filled them to the brim.

Then he told them, 'Now draw some out and take it to the master of the banquet.'

They did so, and the master of the banquet tasted the water that had been turned into wine. He did not realise where it had come from, though the servants who had drawn the water knew. Then he called the bridegroom aside and said, 'Everyone brings out the choice wine first and then the cheaper wine after the guests have had too much to drink; but you have saved the best till now.' (John 2.1–10 NIV)

13. IMAGE

INTRODUCTION

I'm almost positive that when I was a teenager I had no more than two of each item of clothing: two pairs of jeans (straight with a high waistband), two short-sleeved t-shirts, two long-sleeved t-shirts, two jumpers and, I'm not proud to admit, two pairs of underpants. I just didn't need any more than that. Clearly time has done things to my memory – I must have owned more and I'm certain I was more image conscious than I give myself credit for – but it does seem that image, more than ever before, has become an enormous issue for young people. An article in *Retail Week* in 2012 suggested that the growth in fashion in the UK has been meteoric since the days of the relatively simple fare on offer even as recently as the 1990s: in 2011 retail sales in the clothing sector reached £37.9 bn.[1]

For young people image is dictated by so much more than just the clothes they wear. What music they listen to, the TV shows they watch, the car their parents drive and of course the technology they use can all have a massive effect on their image and the way they're perceived by their peers. And when you take into account the incredibly high value they place on image and social capital, you quickly realize why these things matter so much to the members of your group.

This session isn't going to solve all of your young people's image problems! However, it may help you set the scene for them to view themselves a little as God does – his children and made in his image.

LEARNING OUTCOMES

By the end of this session your group will have:

- considered to what extent they're hung up on their image;
- encountered how God views them;
- spent some time thinking how they can keep their self-image in perspective.

OPENING WORSHIP

Use one of the ideas from pages 21–2 or the idea below.

MIRROR IMAGES

This is an activity I've used several times before. It takes a bit of preparation but is worth the effort. You'll need to get two mirrors – preferably identical – and a sheet of transparent sticky-back plastic film big enough to cover one of them. Leave one of the mirrors as it is but cover the second with the film and then, with a hammer, very carefully hit the mirror – only just hard enough to shatter it. The plastic should keep all the pieces together. You'll end up with two mirrors: one that will give a perfect image; one that will give a shattered distorted image. If you're worried about using a broken mirror, use an unbroken one but cover it with enough cling film that the image is visible but distorted – but, exercising all due caution, it's worth giving the shattered mirror a go as the results are quite stunning.

Place the broken mirror on a table and invite the group to come up one at a time and look at their reflection. As they do, read these words:

Today we're going to think about image – how we see ourselves and how we think others see us. How do you feel about your image?

When everyone has looked in the broken mirror, pass the unbroken mirror around the group and read these words:

So God created humankind in his image, in the image of God he created them; male and female he created them. (Genesis 1.27)

If you aren't able to use the broken mirror idea, replace it instead with something that gives a distorted reflection – a magnifying shaving mirror, a stainless steel saucepan lid or even some shiny foil stretched across a cardboard frame. Essentially, anything that gives a false or twisted image of the viewer will do. If you have access to an iPad then the Photo Booth app is a great way to get all sorts of distorted images of your group (equivalent free apps are available on other platforms).

BUSY HANDS

Use one of the activities from page 23 or the idea below.

PERFECT PERSON?

Get a selection of celeb/fashion magazines and some big sheets of paper, and use the images in the magazines to create the 'perfect person'. You may even want to make your own 'e-fit' by taking different features from different people to create a whole new face.

This activity comes with several health warnings. First, you may want to check through the magazines before you hand them out, in case there are any stories or images that might be unsuitable for your particular group. Second, try to steer the conversation away from 'I wish I looked like . . .' Instead, try to focus the group on how we all perceive beauty differently, and point out that the 'perfect face' e-fit actually looks monstrous!

If you prefer, you could simply have a collection of magazines – teen and fitness would be a good mixture – and encourage the group to look at the pictures and adverts and see what they reveal about how people perceive themselves. You could also have some beauty products available: girls' makeup items such as anti-wrinkle cream and lipstick; men's toiletries such as tanning lotion and hair products, and diet or supplement pills.

QUESTIONS TO TALK OVER

- How important would you say image is to people of your age?
- Where do we get our concepts of 'perfect body image'?
- What do you think motivates the people who want us to think that a certain body image is preferable to another?

THE BIBLE BIT

A VERSE

For you created my inmost being;
you knit me together in my mother's womb.
(Psalm 139.13 NIV)

A PASSAGE

Psalm 139.1–4, 13–16

A LONGER READING

Psalm 139

QUESTIONS

- What caught your attention from those words? (Why?)
- What do you think God might be trying to get us to notice?
- How does it feel to be 'known' so completely like this?
- What do you think it means to be 'made in God's image'? Is it possible to be made in God's image and be ugly?
- Can you recognize aspects of God's character in yourself?
- Why do you think so many people have such a low self-image?

NOTICING GOD

Use one of the ideas from pages 25–6 or the idea below.

At the time of writing there's been a stand-off in the media between two famous female pop stars. The young pop star has just released a raunchy, sexually explicit video to accompany her new song and the older pop star has written an open letter to her about the video. Photocopy the extracts from the letter on the next page and ask your group to work through each one and to highlight all of the things that are similar to what God might say.

Once you've completed that activity, invite the group to imagine God writing to them about their own self-image. What kinds of things would he say to them? What advice would he share? Hand out letter paper and pens and give them a few minutes to have a go.

CLOSING

Now all we can see of God
is like a cloudy picture
in a mirror.
Later we will see him
face to face.
We don't know everything,
but then we will,
just as God completely
understands us.
(1 Corinthians 13.12 CEV)

Lord God, we look forward to seeing ourselves as you see us, help us to look for you in our lives and to want to be more like you.

Amen.

LETTER FROM AN OLDER POP STAR TO A YOUNGER POP STAR

I am extremely concerned for you that those around you have led you to believe, or encouraged you in your own belief, that it is in any way 'cool' to be naked and licking sledgehammers in your videos. It is in fact the case that you will obscure your talent by allowing yourself to be pimped, whether it's the music business or yourself doing the pimping.

Nothing but harm will come in the long run, from allowing yourself to be exploited, and it is absolutely NOT in ANY way an empowerment of yourself or any other young women, for you to send across the message that you are to be valued (even by you) more for your sexual appeal than your obvious talent. I am happy to hear I am somewhat of a role model for you and I hope that because of that you will pay close attention to what I am telling you . . . I'm suggesting you don't care for yourself. That has to change. You ought be protected as a precious young lady by anyone in your employ and anyone around you, including you. This is a dangerous world. We don't encourage our daughters to walk around naked in it because it makes them prey for animals and less than animals, a distressing majority of whom work in the music industry and its associated media.

You are worth more than your body or your sexual appeal. The world of showbiz doesn't see things that way, they like things to be seen the other way, whether they are magazines who want you on their cover, or whatever . . . Don't be under any illusions . . . ALL of them want you because they're making money off your youth and your beauty . . . which they could not do except for the fact your youth makes you blind to the evils of show business. If you have an innocent heart you can't recognise those who do not.[2]

14. EXAMS

INTRODUCTION

This session could also be titled 'success' – it will cover the same kinds of issues. We're told that young people are under more stress than ever before and that the drive to succeed, whether at school or elsewhere, is very high. At the time of writing the news is filled with conflicting stories, on the one hand praising young people for getting better results than ever, on the other claiming that exams are easier than in the past and that grades are being 'inflated' by educational establishments keen to boost their position in all-important league tables.

Exams are funny things, especially when as adults we're able to look at them through the perspective of time – I'm glad to say I haven't had to do a quadratic equation since sitting maths GCSE. For a young person facing exams, however, they can seem utterly overwhelming. This session will help them develop a bit of a God perspective on the whole thing, while still encouraging them to have ambition and work hard.

LEARNING OUTCOMES

By the end of this session your group will have:

- thought about what it means to do their best;
- reflected on the idea that God can use any situation for his purpose and glory;
- gained an understanding of God's perspective on success.

OPENING WORSHIP

Use one of the ideas from pages 21–2 or the idea below.

Have a simple wooden cross in the room before the group enters. As they come in, give them each a piece of paper, an envelope and a pen. Ask them to sit in silence for a few moments and then explain that in today's session you're going to be thinking about exams.

Ask them to think for a moment about their future and their plans – what jobs they want to do; whether and where they want to go to university; what other hopes and dreams they have. Ask them to write some of these hopes and plans on the paper – just a few words – and then to seal it up in the envelope.

Invite them to place their envelopes at the cross then read these words:

> *'. . . I know the plans I have for you,' declares the LORD, 'plans to prosper you and not to harm you, plans to give you hope and a future.'*
>
> *(Jeremiah 29.11 NIV)*

After a few more moments, quietly move on with the session.

BUSY HANDS

Use one of the activities from page 23 or the idea below.

As you'll see, you'll need various things for this section.

There is a concept, particularly from days gone by, that we should give our 'utmost for his highest' – in other words, 'only the best is good enough for God'. Contemporary Christianity shies away from spending vast amounts on creating beautiful things for God, but historically, in many traditions, creating something fabulous and expensive for God was considered a wonderful act of worship. It's why we have such beautiful church buildings filled with exquisite works of art.

This session's activity will get the group to think about what it means to give of our best as an act of worship, while trying to create something beautiful of their own.

Have pictures available of some of our more famous and beautiful cathedrals and churches – you could start with Winchester, Lincoln and Salisbury cathedrals and go from there. Also have some pictures of the more famous pieces of religious art – try doing an online image search for Michelangelo's painting on the ceiling of the Sistine chapel, for example, or have a look at Salvador Dali's painting *Christ of St John of the Cross*. If you fancy something more contemporary there's a really moving video clip on YouTube of Matisse's Chapelle du Rosaire in Vence, France – http://youtu.be/APaXLXAVkmQ. No doubt you have your own favourites that you could share with your group. If you want to go all out, why not play some choral music too – Allegri's *Miserere* is bound to give you goosebumps!

Give everyone a bar of soap (the really cheap own-brand stuff from supermarkets is fine and actually carves better than expensive soap), along with a selection of carving tools (knives, forks and spoons are all good), and get them to carve something beautiful, inspired by what they see and what they hear.

QUESTIONS TO TALK OVER

- How do you feel about your exams?
- What do you think your attitude to studying should be if you're a Christian? Why?
- Some people might say that as God is in control, there's no use trying in exams because he has a plan for you and so will sort it all out regardless of your results. What do you think about that?

THE BIBLE BIT

A VERSE

I can do all this through him who gives me strength.' *(Philippians 4.13* NIV*)*

A PASSAGE

Philippians 4.4–9

A LONGER READING

Philippians 4

QUESTIONS

I often hear young people – Christian or otherwise – subscribing to the view that 'everything happens for a reason'. Personally I don't recognize this as the way God works or as a Christian teaching as such. Rather, I think God can use every situation for his purpose or for the good of those who love him – that's a rough interpretation of Romans 8.28, 'And we know that in all things God works for the good of those who love him' (NIV).

As you work through these questions and reflect on the reading, bear that thought in mind – it's helpful because it doesn't allow us just to hand over all responsibility to God but it does mean that God continues to work for our good even when things seem to have gone wrong.

- What caught your attention from these words? (Why?)
- What do you think God might be trying to get us to notice?
- What do we achieve by getting stressed about exams?
- Is success a godly attribute? (Discuss!)
- Is there a tension between doing our best and trusting in God?

NOTICING GOD

Use one of the ideas from pages 25–6 or the idea below.

In advance of the session prepare a large sheet of paper or cardboard with a target drawn on it. At the centre of the target copy these words from Ecclesiastes:

What is the best thing to do in the short life that God has given us? I think we should enjoy eating, drinking, and working hard. This is what God intends for us to do. Suppose you are very rich and able to enjoy everything you own. Then go ahead and enjoy working hard – this is God's gift to you. God will keep you so happy that you won't have time to worry about each day.
(Ecclesiastes 5.18–20 CEV)

If the group wrote down their ambitions as the opening worship for this session, now would be the time to distribute the envelopes back to their owners. Encourage the group to open the envelopes and to fold the sheets into aeroplanes and then throw them at the target you've prepared. When they go to collect their planes, get someone to read the words from Ecclesiastes written on the target.

Ask them whether their ambitions fit with this very simple guidance from the Old Testament.

CLOSING

By wisdom the LORD laid the earth's
foundations,
by understanding he set the heavens in place;
by his knowledge the watery depths were
divided,
and the clouds let drop the dew.
(Proverbs 3.19–20 NIV)

Help me to remember that however complex the subject may be that I am tackling, you can enable me to grasp it, understand it and remember the details because you are the originator of all knowledge.[1]

Amen.

15. BUSYNESS

INTRODUCTION

One in ten young people (10 per cent) feel they cannot cope with day-to-day life, warns The Prince's Trust Youth Index.[1]

We're getting used to seeing statistics like these in the media. By all accounts, while many adults think young people have never had it so good, young people seem to be feeling higher and higher levels of stress. The UK may no longer be bottom of the table in UNICEF's report on children's well-being, but we're still rated sixteenth out of the 21 most developed countries in the world – not something we can really boast about.[2] While there are all sorts of factors contributing to these feelings (including fear of unemployment and the difficulties posed by the internet and social media), there's also a problem with young people and busyness. Expectations on them to work harder at school, to pursue out-of-school activities, alongside an 'always-connected' culture where messages and information are readily accessible 24/7, means that young people have very little downtime. And that's just those who aren't plugged into a church. Christian young people may well be worshipping on Sundays, attending one or more youth sessions each week as well as helping in children's groups or the sound desk or playing in the worship band – no wonder they're so tired and grumpy all the time!

Add into that mix recent scientific research that points to young people needing longer sleep than many of them get,[3] and the need for them to be able to sleep later, and you've got a recipe for disaster – it's just possible that your young people need some space!

I'm acutely conscious that busyness is often seen as a badge of honour for those of us in ministry. When asked how we are we automatically reply 'Busy'. We often boast about the hours we've worked in a week or make comments about people who pursue hobbies – 'I'd love to have the time to do something like that . . .'. We're the masters of our own destinies, and if we want young people to grow up pursuing balanced lives then we, as their leaders, need to model that.

How is your work–life balance?

This session, then, is designed to help your group examine their lives and consider how busy they are, and to explore the impact modern life might be having on them. It gives them space to relax and chill and to consider ways they can confront busyness. Lastly, it touches on the idea of Sabbath – that God at the moment of creation, and Jesus before each day, took time out to be, to rest and to pray.

LEARNING OUTCOMES

By the end of this session your group will have:

- considered how busy they are;
- reflected on some biblical practices of finding space and quiet;
- had a go at some ways of slowing themselves down.

OPENING WORSHIP

Use one of the ideas from pages 21–2 or the idea below.

This opening activity is lifted directly from the NHS website – it's a long, slow deep muscle relaxation. Feel free to use the activity straight as it is, or if you want to increase the group's awareness of God while they do the activity, you could play some gentle worship music. Or, when they're completely relaxed, you could read them a Bible passage that reminds them of God's love for them – Psalm 139 would be ideal (although you may want to skip verses 19–22!).

DEEP MUSCLE RELAXATION

This technique takes around 20 minutes. It stretches different muscles in turn and then relaxes them, to release tension from the body and relax your mind.

Find a warm, quiet place with no distractions. Get completely comfortable, either sitting or lying down. Close your eyes and begin by focusing on your breathing; breathing slowly and deeply, as described above.

If you have pain in certain muscles, or if there are muscles that you find it difficult to focus on, spend more time on relaxing other parts.

You may want to play some soothing music to help relaxation. As with all relaxation techniques, deep muscle relaxation will require a bit of practice before you start feeling its benefits.

For each exercise, hold the stretch for a few seconds, then relax. Repeat it a couple of times. It's useful to keep to the same order as you work through the muscle groups:

- Face: push the eyebrows together, as though frowning, then release.
- Neck: gently tilt the head forwards, pushing chin down towards chest, then slowly lift again.
- Shoulders: pull them up towards the ears (shrug), then relax them down towards the feet.
- Chest: breathe slowly and deeply into the diaphragm (below your bottom rib) so that you're using the whole of the lungs. Then breathe slowly out, allowing the belly to deflate as all the air is exhaled.
- Arms: stretch the arms away from the body, reach, then relax.
- Legs: push the toes away from the body, then pull them towards the body, then relax.
- Wrists and hands: stretch the wrist by pulling the hand up towards you, and stretch out the fingers and thumbs, then relax.

Spend some time lying quietly after your relaxation with your eyes closed. When you feel ready, stretch and get up slowly.[4]

BUSY HANDS

It may seem ironic in a session on busyness to have a **Busy hands** activity, but one of the key ways to help young people overcome stress is to talk things through, and as we've already discovered, we all talk more easily when we've got something to do to distract us. So, use one of the activities from page 23 or the idea below.

CHOCOLATE TRUFFLES

There's possibly nothing more relaxing that crashing on a sofa, sticking your feet up and eating chocolate – preferably with good friends to chat to! It's up to you how much preparation you do with this activity before the group arrives – if time is limitless then start from scratch; if not, have the truffle mixture ready-made and chilled and get your group to do the shaping, rolling and coating (and eating!).

- Melt 280g good quality dark chocolate in small pieces over barely simmering water.
- Allow the chocolate to cool a little while you let a 284ml pot of double cream come to room temperature.
- Whisk the cream into the chocolate a little at a time until the mixture begins to thicken – this will add a lightness to the truffles.
- Cover the mixture and place in the fridge for between 30 minutes and 1 hour to firm up.
- Take teaspoons of the mixture, roll them between the palms or your hands and then roll them in your selected coatings. Be as creative as you like with these: you could use crushed biscuits or meringue, chopped nuts (check for allergies), cocoa powder or icing sugar, edible glitter, vermicelli, hundreds and thousands – whatever takes your fancy. If you want to go super posh you could have bowls of melted dark, milk and white chocolate and then, using cocktail sticks, dip the truffles into them and leave them on non-stick baking parchment to set.
- Chill before serving. (You may want to save them for the **Noticing God** section of the session later.)

QUESTIONS TO TALK OVER

- In a typical week, when do you feel most relaxed?
- In a typical week, when do you feel most stressed?
- When you're stressed, what do you do to relax?

THE BIBLE BIT

TWO VERSES

'Martha, Martha,' the Lord answered, 'you are worried and upset about many things, but few things are needed – or indeed only one. Mary has chosen what is better, and it will not be taken away from her.' (Luke 10.41–42 NIV)

A PASSAGE

Luke 10.38–42

A LONGER READING

Luke 10.38–42 and Matthew 11.28–30

QUESTIONS

- What caught your attention from these words? (Why?)
- What do you think God might be trying to get us to notice?
- Who do you relate to? Mary or Martha?
- Do you think Jesus is telling us not to do housework?
- In the passage Jesus approves of Mary sitting at his feet and listening to him. What other things do you think Jesus might want to encourage us to do?

NOTICING GOD

Use one of the ideas from pages 25–6 or the idea below.

SLEEPING LIONS (EATING CHOCOLATE TRUFFLES)

If you made chocolate truffles earlier, now is a good time to put them to use. If not, have a couple of bars of chocolate ready to hand – you'll need solid chocolate. If you fancy it, why not use good quality chocolate and do a proper chocolate tasting.

Give each of the group a chocolate truffle or a piece of chocolate. Encourage them to find somewhere really comfortable where they can sit or lie and totally relax.

Explain that at your signal they're to put the chocolate in their mouths and then, without chewing, let it slowly melt. They're not allowed to move or speak until the chocolate has completely gone. Ask them to think about the flavours of the chocolate, the textures and the sensations as it melts.

After a couple of minutes take round a second piece of chocolate or a second truffle. Ask the group to repeat the activity, but this time read these words:

By the seventh day God had finished the work he had been doing; so on the seventh day he rested from all his work. (Genesis 2.2 NIV)

While it was still night, way before dawn, he got up and went out to a secluded spot and prayed. (Mark 1.35 THE MESSAGE)

After the work of creating the universe, God rested.
Before the toil of each day, Jesus took time out.

When do you stop?
When do you seek God?
What does he say to you?

When you feel enough time has passed, and before the group gets restless, invite them to get up and return to their chairs. Feel free to finish the chocolate.

CLOSING

Use your regular closing prayer or the following words if you prefer:

Jesus said 'Come to me, all you who are weary and burdened, and I will give you rest.' (Matthew 11.28 NIV)

Help us Lord God to find space in the busyness, to stop, to wait and to hear from you.

Amen.

16. SEXUALITY

INTRODUCTION

Young people are talking about sex and they're talking about sexuality. The idea that it's a taboo subject that simply can't be addressed is no longer the case. But Christian young people may be torn between two polarized views. Some will believe vehemently that homosexuality is a sin, while for others there'll be a genuine disgust with a Church that can't just accept that 'Some people are gay. Get over it', to quote from a 2009 Stonewall anti-homophobia campaign.

At a theological level we need to make space for young people to explore this issue, unpacking whether homosexuality is part of a God-given image or a choice we make influenced by the world and the culture we find ourselves in.

At the time of writing there's a very neat little video clip doing the rounds on Facebook – see http://youtu.be/8TJxnYgP6D8. It shows the reactions of a group of American children – not necessarily from a faith background – to two different gay-marriage proposals. It's well worth watching if you want an insight into the minds of young people thinking about homosexuality. While the video isn't by any means a piece of scientific research, I think it's an excellent summing up of the shared views of many young people in our culture, and it gives a good hint at what the future will look like concerning the way gay people are accepted in our societies.

This won't necessarily be a straightforward session! Prepare to have your views challenged – and your opinions changed. And be willing to listen to the views of your group. Also be aware that there'll almost certainly be members who are confused about their own sexuality or exploring their sexual identity – so tread carefully.

LEARNING OUTCOMES

By the end of this session your group will have:

- thought about what it means to be in love;
- considered some of the biblical texts on the subject of love and sexuality;
- reflected on their own sexuality and how they treat others who may feel differently.

OPENING WORSHIP

Use one of the ideas from pages 21–2 or the idea below.

Set the scene for this session by looking at the words from 1 Corinthians about love.

> *Love is patient, love is kind. It does not envy, it does not boast, it is not proud. It does not dishonour others, it is not self-seeking, it is not easily angered, it keeps no record of wrongs. Love does not delight in evil but rejoices with the truth. It always protects, always trusts, always hopes, always perseveres. Love never fails.* (1 Corinthians 13.4–8a NIV)

For a creative retelling of these well-known words, use the video at www.rethinkworship.com/love-life-1-corinthians-13/.

Share round a packet of love hearts and lead your group in a short prayer like the one below.

Lord God, as we try to get to grips with a difficult subject, help us to know your love above all things. Help us to treat each other with grace, to listen without judging and to speak without condemning. Let us know your presence, we pray.

Amen.

BUSY HANDS

Use one of the activities from page 23 or the idea below.

This will take a little preparation. You need to get hold of some string, rope or electric cable that's become tangled and knotted. Dump it in the middle of your group and set them the task of getting it untangled. Don't make it too easy, and don't worry if they can't get it completely untangled – that will help prove the point!

Rather than have the usual questions section at this point, move straight into the Bible section.

THE BIBLE BIT

This is a bit of a departure from the usual **Bible bit** sections and is aimed at getting the group to think about love and what it means to love someone. The first two passages are meant to show two different kinds of love: the passionate love between two young lovers and the love two men can have for one another. The readings are deliberately a little contentious in that the 1 Samuel passage is often used to defend homosexual attraction and the Genesis one to condemn it. I don't think either passage is as clear cut as that – you should expect some interesting discussion!

'THE MAN' AND 'THE WOMAN' IN THE SONG OF SOLOMON

THE WOMAN

Kiss me – full on the mouth!
Yes! For your love is better than wine,
headier than your aromatic oils.
The syllables of your name murmur like a meadow brook.
No wonder everyone loves to say your name!

THE MAN

Dear, dear friend and lover,
you're as beautiful as Tirzah, city of delights,
Lovely as Jerusalem, city of dreams,
the ravishing visions of my ecstasy.
Your beauty is too much for me – I'm in over my head.
I'm not used to this! I can't take it in.'
(Song of Solomon 1.2–3 and 6.4–5 THE MESSAGE)

DAVID AND JONATHAN

Jonathan became one in spirit with David, and he loved him as himself. From that day Saul kept David with him and did not let him return home to his family. And Jonathan made a covenant with David because he loved him as himself. Jonathan took off the robe he was wearing and gave it to David, along with his tunic, and even his sword, his bow and his belt.
(1 Samuel 18.1b–4 NIV)

QUESTIONS

- What caught your attention from these words? (Why?)
- What do you think God might be trying to get us to notice?

- Which of these passages most touched you? Why?
- What do these different kinds of love have in common? How are they different?
- Some people believe David and Jonathan were lovers. Why do you think we might jump to that conclusion?

Now read these words to your group from Genesis:

That is why a man leaves his father and mother and is united to his wife, and they become one flesh. *(Genesis 2.24 NIV)*

QUESTIONS

- Some Christians say that this verse outlines God's 'ideal' for sexual relationships – that is, within marriage and between one man and one woman. Do you think sexual activity should be confined to marriage between a man and a woman?
- If so, what would you say to someone who can only love and desire people of their own sex?

NOTICING GOD

Use one of the ideas from pages 25–6 or the idea below.

OLD ENOUGH TO DECIDE

Have available some pictures that will remind your group of when they were little children – think about the TV shows they'd have watched, the games they might have played or clothes they'd have worn. You want to get them reminiscing.

Also have available a timeline with the numbers 0–25 written on it, and some pieces of paper or card with the following activities written or printed out:

- what clothes to wear
- fall in love
- control of your own money
- driving
- when to go to bed
- having sex
- knowing if you're gay or straight
- staying out after 10 p.m.
- choosing you own lunch
- watching an 18-rated film
- playing an 18-rated video game
- smoking
- drinking alcohol

Feel free to add more to your list if you want. Once your group has had a chance to reminisce for a while, invite them to place the activity cards on the timeline, according to what they think is appropriate for each age. As ever, don't push anyone to get involved if they don't want to, and don't force the conversation.

CLOSING

Finish this session by simply sharing the peace[1] with each other around the group. Encourage the group to share the words with all the other members, and to shake hands or hug, if that's appropriate. Explain that this prayer is about setting aside differences and disagreements, and approaching God as a family.

Leader The peace of the Lord be always with you

All **and also with you.**

Leader Let us offer one another a sign of peace.

17. SCIENCE

INTRODUCTION

It's safe to say that there exists a disconnect between science and faith. For most of us this probably isn't deliberate. The part of the Church that maintains that the two are incompatible remains relatively small, but for a large majority of us, mostly due to a lack of confidence in the subject, we remain quiet, and our silence creates a chasm. The Barna Group did some research with young people and youth leaders in the USA and discovered that while 51 per cent of students were planning on a future career in a science-based subject, only 1 per cent of youth leaders had addressed issues of science in the previous 12 months.[1] Meanwhile fashionable scientists like Brian Cox and Richard Dawkins, often with strong atheistic views, are regularly on the airwaves raising the image of science and often treading down religious faith.

One of the marks of discipleship is the ability to discover God in all aspects of life. We often compartmentalize worship as the thing we do in church on a Sunday – perhaps that's why it's often difficult to have conversations about faith and science, because we don't equate the cerebral activity of intellectual discourse with the music- and art-focused activity of worship that we're used to. In his book *Sacred Pathways*, Gary Thomas lists nine common ways that Christians can engage with God. My heart sank as I ploughed through the first eight – they were all good and worthy routes to spirituality but none made my heart sing. So it was with great relief that I found Thomas' final pathway, 'Intellectuals'. Don't get me wrong: I don't claim to be an intellectual, but I can totally relate to these words:

> *Intellectuals need their minds to be stirred before their hearts come truly alive. They are likely to be studying (and, in some instances, arguing either for or against) topics such as Calvinism, infant baptism, ordination of women, and predestination. These Christians live in the world of concepts. Some intellectuals, influenced by a personality type that is shy or withdrawn, might avoid intellectual confrontation but still be 'fed' primarily by intellectual activity. 'Faith' is something to be understood as much as experienced. They may feel closest to God when they first understand something new about him.*[2]

My firmly held belief is that there's no such thing as a science–faith choice, and I've met enough excellent scientists who are Christians to give me confidence that the two aren't incompatible. Rather I think we're creatures of wonder and thoughtful enquiry, and it's those two things that can lead us so easily into a place of worship. What I do struggle with, and what I think turns many young people off the Christian faith, is when our teaching stops us wondering by giving us answers, instead of giving us the opportunity to discover for ourselves.

While the basis of this session is an opportunity to look at science, it really goes much wider than that. So rather than giving you the opportunity to have a go at the old creation vs evolution argument again, think of this more as a chance for you and your group to grow in the confidence that it's all right to have a Christian faith in the face of aggressive atheism and science.

LEARNING OUTCOMES

By the end of this session your group will have:

- wondered at the glory of God's creation;
- confronted the idea that science and faith are incompatible;
- discovered new forms of inquiry.

OPENING WORSHIP

ENQUIRING MINDS

Building on Gary Thomas' idea that intellectual discourse can be a pathway to spirituality, this opening activity gives your group the chance to thrash out some big ideas about faith and science. Photocopy or write out the statements on p. 85 on separate pieces of paper or card so that everyone in your group can see each of the quotes. Invite them to choose which statement they feel most comfortable with and then to choose if they want to offer an argument supporting their choice.

Be careful to avoid this getting into personal arguing or fighting. Encourage your group to stick to the facts on their sheet and to discuss the concepts with each other rather than each others' beliefs or views.

BUSY HANDS

Use one of the activities from page 23 or the idea below.

MAKING MOLECULES

You'll need a big box of cocktails sticks (or several boxes, depending on the size of your group) and a box of soaked (but not cooked) dried peas. You might also want to have available some pictures of molecule models (an online image search will find plenty of these). Using the peas to stick the cocktail sticks together, get your group to try and make the most complicated molecule models they can. The beauty of this activity is that when the peas dry, they set pretty solid, meaning you can keep the models when they're made.

QUESTIONS TO TALK OVER

- Which do you enjoy more, science-based subjects or arts? Why?
- How do you feel when someone asks you a question and you don't know the answer?
- Do you think you can be a scientist and a Christian?

THE BIBLE BIT

Unsurprisingly, it's difficult to find Bible stories of scientists. The creation story is often cited as a reason not to believe in the God of the Bible, and although there are scientists in there (Luke the physician being the obvious one), it's difficult to pin down particular passages that point to a good relationship between science and faith, despite Luke's methodical analytical style. So I thought we might look at the story of Daniel. I think it's relevant for a couple of reasons: first because the Babylonians were a scientifically advanced race (relatively speaking), and I get the feeling Daniel would have attracted many of the labels people of faith attract these days. But mostly I think it's relevant because it talks of an intelligent young man, immersed in a foreign culture in which he had to learn the language and literature of that culture, who not only survived but indeed flourished. Although this may take some explanation for your group, I think it's worth the effort for them to discover that living in a society more technologically advanced than your own doesn't mean you have to disappear into a corner and disown all your beliefs.

TWO VERSES

Then the king ordered Ashpenaz, chief of his court officials, to bring into the king's service some of the Israelites from the royal family and the nobility – young men without any physical defect, handsome, showing aptitude for every kind of learning, well informed, quick to understand, and qualified to serve in the king's palace. He was to teach them the language and literature of the Babylonians. The king assigned them a daily amount of food and wine from the king's table. They were to be trained for three years, and after that they were to enter the king's service. *(Daniel 1.3–5 NIV)*

A PASSAGE

Daniel 1.1–21

A LONGER READING

The book of Daniel!

QUESTIONS

- What caught your attention from these words? (Why?)
- What do you think God might be trying to get us to notice?
- What kind of person do you think Daniel was? Would you have liked him?
- Can you relate to his situation? In what ways?
- How can we have a foot in the science of our culture but, like Daniel, still remain true to God?

NOTICING GOD

Use one of the ideas from pages 25–6 or the idea below.

You'll need to prepare a pile of nature pictures – you could chop up a few old magazines, pull apart a few suitable calendars or do what I did and buy a packet of 10 cm x 15 cm glossy photo sheets and spend a couple of hours searching online for photos of nature – mountains, oceans, sunsets, polar bears and the like – and printing them out.

Spread the pictures on the floor and invite your group to walk around looking at them and then to pick up the picture that most speaks to them. If anyone is comfortable, ask them to share why they've chosen a particular picture.

You could play some music in the background if you think it would help – maybe 'How great thou art', or if you prefer something more contemporary, maybe 'Indescribable' by Jesse Reeves and Laura Story or 'Creation Sings the Father's Song' by Keith Getty, Kristyn Getty and Stuart Townend.

CLOSING

Dear Lord

It seems unlikely that we will ever find conclusive answers to our biggest science questions about the creation of the universe, the origin of life or what preceded it all. Help us to seek your face above all else, and to trust that you are the God of all things.

Amen.

Science is not only compatible with spirituality; it is a profound source of spirituality. When we recognize our place in an immensity of light-years and in the passage of ages, when we grasp the intricacy, beauty, and subtlety of life, then that soaring feeling, that sense of elation and humility combined, is surely spiritual.

Carl Sagan[3]

The Bible should be taught, but emphatically not as reality. It is fiction, myth, poetry, anything but reality. As such it needs to be taught because it underlies so much of our literature and our culture. *Richard Dawkins*[4]

This most beautiful system of the sun, planets and comets, could only proceed from the counsel and dominion of an intelligent and powerful Being.

Isaac Newton[5]

People often ask me, 'OK, do you believe in creation or God?' And I always say quite honestly, how we got to be who we are is so much less important than getting together to get ourselves out of this horrendous mess that we have put the planet in. We're reaching the point of no return. We've got to roll up our sleeves. We've got to take action. We can't afford to sit back and philosophize too long about how we got to be the way we are.

Jane Goodall[6]

I find religion and science present no conflict. Both proceed from acts of faith. The religious follower holds that the universe evolves according to God's plan. The scientist believes that a few fundamental and potentially comprehensible principles can explain the mechanism he observes in the universe.

Robert A. Naumann[7]

Thus the heavens and the earth were completed in all their vast array. By the seventh day God had finished the work he had been doing; so on the seventh day he rested from all his work. Then God blessed the seventh day and made it holy, because on it he rested from all the work of creating that he had done.

(Genesis 2.1–3 NIV*)*

I can never prove to somebody else the satisfaction that the god that I perceive is not simply a figment of my imagination. But I personally don't believe that I have invented God.

Jocelyn Bell Burnell[8]

The laws which enable the universe to come into being spontaneously seem themselves to be the product of exceedingly ingenious design. If physics is the product of design, the universe must have a purpose.

Paul Davies[9]

18. PORNOGRAPHY

INTRODUCTION

In the media there seems to be something of a divide about this subject. For the most part people seem pretty united in their opposition to the influence of pornography over our society, and in particular its effect on young people and children.[1] Needless to say, there's also the view from some that this is another 'moral panic' and that perhaps there isn't anything to worry about.[2]

While it's true we don't have any solid evidence on what the actual risks are to young people's development, I think we can be pretty sure that the proliferation of pornography through the media, particularly via the internet but also through so much of the music industry, is having a damaging effect – on young people's development, on their attitude towards sex and on the way young men in particular view women.

You can be pretty certain that young people in your group have come into contact with pornography in one form or another, and that some of them may well be involved in creating so-called 'user-generated content' – sexually explicit selfies and so on.[3]

This session aims to help you have an open conversation about pornography, highlighting some of the issues associated with its use and providing a safe space for the group to talk openly about their habits and struggles. You may want to divide your group by gender for this session – so that both sexes feel confident to talk about their experiences.

LEARNING OUTCOMES

By the end of this session your group will have:

- considered a biblical view on sex and its relation to the use of pornography;
- had an opportunity to talk about their own thoughts and experiences of pornography;
- thought about some of the effects of using pornography.

OPENING WORSHIP

If possible, watch the *Honda Illusions* advert on YouTube, at http://youtu.be/UeIJZG_bF98 – there's also a 'behind the scenes' version at http://youtu.be/ejXgE480R1I. Otherwise have some well-known optical-illusion pictures printed out for the group to see – you could blow these up and have them on the walls or even just on a table for them to sit around – there's a good archive available at http://brainden.com/optical-illusions.htm.

Read these words from 1 Corinthians and then the prayer below. Allow a short time for silence.

There's more to sex than mere skin on skin. Sex is as much spiritual mystery as physical fact. As written in Scripture, 'The two become one.' Since we want to become spiritually one with the Master, we must not pursue the kind of sex that avoids commitment and intimacy, leaving us more lonely than ever – the kind of sex that can never 'become one.'

(1 Corinthians 6.16–17 THE MESSAGE*)*

Lord God, as we talk about a tricky subject in our time together, help us to hear your voice and to know your will. Sometimes the world offers us things that seem so tempting, and yet we know they can never satisfy. Help us to see through the optical illusion of pornography, which seems to offer fulfilment but will only leave us 'more lonely than ever'.

Amen.

BUSY HANDS

Use one of the activities from page 23 or the idea below.

You can use this activity to help the group talk about the difference between real and fake, to compare the enjoyment offered by the quick sugary fix of sweets and the long-term benefit of a healthy diet. This activity will lead into the Bible discussion.

SUGAR, FRUIT AND VEG

You'll need a packet of white royal icing (or white marzipan), food colouring and paintbrushes. Using the icing or marzipan, mould pieces of miniature fruit and veg and use the food colouring and paintbrushes to decorate them. Do an online image search for 'marzipan fruit' if you need inspiration.

QUESTIONS TO TALK OVER

- Would eating these fruit and veg count towards our five-a-day? Why not?
- Singers often portray themselves in a highly sexualized way for their music videos; TV celebs will pose naked for magazines to boost their careers. Why is this do you think?
- Why is internet pornography so popular? Why do people find it so alluring?

THE BIBLE BIT

A VERSE

Flee from sexual immorality. All other sins a person commits are outside the body, but whoever sins sexually, sins against their own body. *(1 Corinthians 6.18* NIV*)*

A PASSAGE

1 Corinthians 6.12–20

A LONGER READING

1 Corinthians 6.12—7.9

QUESTIONS

- What caught your attention from these words? Why?
- What do you think God might be trying to get us to notice?
- How do we differentiate between what feels good and what is good for us?
- The implication from this passage is that sexual sin is somehow more harmful than other sin because it's a sin against your own body. What do you think that means?
- Verses 19–20 of the 1 Corinthians passage say: 'You are not your own; you were bought at a price.' What do you think that means?
- What's that got to do with sex/pornography?

NOTICING GOD

Use one of the ideas from pages 25–6 or the idea below.

Visit www.stopobjectification.com, run by fashion designer Norma Kalani. She encourages women to take photos of their strongest or favourite body part and to write an empowering caption about what it is that makes them strong. Talk about your group's favourite body part or attribute – you could invite them to use their phones to take a selfie of their 'strongest body part' if they want to. Now give each of them a sticky label and get them to think about the 'empowering caption' they might want to write across their picture – use examples from www.stopobjectification.com if you need inspiration.

Now read this from 1 John:

> *See what love the Father has given us, that we should be called children of God; and that is what we are.* *(1 John 3.1)*

If they haven't already written something similar, invite the group to write the words 'Child of God' over their sticker. Give them a new sticker if there's no space on the original.

Explain that one of the biggest issues with pornography is that it reduces the people depicted to objects to be used, rather than recognizing them as God's children.

How can we become better at seeing other people as God's creations rather than as objects?

CLOSING

Before you read this session's closing prayer below, you may want to spend a moment letting your group know that if any of them are struggling with an addiction to pornography, they can speak to you or to another member of the team. Explain that pornography is a difficult habit to break and that talking about it with someone is always the best place to start.

Even if good people fall seven times, they will get back up. (Proverbs 24.16 CEV)

Help us, Lord God, to be the kind of people who come back to you when we fall. Help us to see you in everyone we meet and see, recognizing God's children.

Amen.

19. SUFFERING

INTRODUCTION

On the day I write this, the war in Syria rages, families in China wait in agony for news of their loved ones missing after a plane has vanished, and we remember the tsunami and earthquake that caused devastation in Japan three years ago. You could argue that it's just a normal news day, so it shouldn't come as any surprise that, just as they have for hundreds of years, young Christians ask how a God of love can allow such awful suffering.

It's unlikely that in this session you'll find any satisfactory answers for your group; in fact I've put off writing this session until the very end because in truth I simply don't know what to write. Don't get me wrong: I know all the philosophical answers; I can argue the sound biblical and theological truths. But if I'm completely honest, they don't really make any difference. I'm still at a loss. It still doesn't seem fair. So while you'll have a chance to think about suffering, and a Christian response, ultimately you'll have to rest on that most wonderful of Christian answers: 'I just don't know'.

Why does God allow earthquakes? Why did my mum have to die? How could God create such evil people? I just don't know.

LEARNING OUTCOMES

By the end of this session your group will have:

- considered the source of evil and suffering in our world;
- thought about what God's response to suffering is;
- talked about their role in responding to suffering.

OPENING WORSHIP

Give everyone in the group a piece of clay or some Play-Doh® and then invite them to model something beautiful. You may want to have made a flower or something similar in advance, or to have some pictures of beautiful sculptures for them to see as examples.

Don't spend too long, but encourage them to put in some effort and to really try and make something special.

As they create, read these words from Genesis 1:

> ***God saw all that he had made, and it was very good.*** *(Genesis 1.31 NIV)*

Once they've all created something, ask them to share what they've made around the room so that everyone holds someone else's creation. Once they've all swapped round, ask the group to admire what their friend has created – and then to slowly and deliberately destroy what they now hold in their hands.

Ask the group how they feel – both seeing their creation destroyed and destroying someone else's. With a bit of luck you'll have all sorts of reactions – shrieks of disappointment, whoops of laughter, refusals even to take part.

BUSY HANDS

Use one of the activities from page 23 or the idea below.

You'll need a big sheet of paper, newspapers and some sticky notes. If you want, you can go through the newspapers and cut out pictures and stories that depict suffering, trying to find a range of different experiences – from losing a pet (local papers are often good for this) to some of the big world disasters. You may need to search online for pictures of specific events and print them off, depending on what the papers are focusing on that week. Be ready to explain any of the stories the group hasn't come across.

On the big sheet of paper write 'Massive' at the top and 'Small' at the bottom. Invite the group to try and sort the pictures into a kind of ranking of suffering.

Once they're agreed (could take a while!), write 'Caused by people' on the right-hand side of the sheet and 'Just happened' on the other side. Can they now move the pictures to depict what caused the suffering? Encourage them to think this through – while an earthquake is clearly a natural disaster, much of the suffering is caused by poverty and poor housing which, it could be argued, is suffering caused by people.[1]

QUESTIONS TO TALK OVER

You'll probably find that there's plenty to talk about as you continue with this activity, but if conversation is proving difficult, you could try asking:

- Why do we think of some kinds of suffering as worse than others?
- Why do we sometimes feel we should take other peoples' suffering more seriously than our own?
- Why is it that sometimes, when we see or hear about someone's suffering, it makes us groan or feel unwell?

THE BIBLE BIT

TWO VERSES

Praise be to the God and Father of our Lord Jesus Christ, the Father of compassion and the God of all comfort, who comforts us in all our troubles, so that we can comfort those in any trouble with the comfort we ourselves receive from God. (2 Corinthians 1.3–4 NIV)

A PASSAGE

2 Corinthians 1.3–7

A LONGER READING

2 Corinthians 1.3–11

QUESTIONS

- What caught your attention from these words? Why?
- What do you think God might be trying to get us to notice?
- Does this passage give you comfort or disturb you? Why?
- How do we feel God's comfort when we experience troubles?
- What kinds of things can we do to comfort others who have troubles?

NOTICING GOD

Use one of the ideas from pages 25–6 or the idea below.

Return to the big sheet of paper from the **Busy hands** section above, and ask your group to have a look at it for a moment. Which of the stories catch their attention? Which are they most moved by?

Invite them to be quiet for a moment and then to pray for God to speak to them about how they could respond to that suffering – use these words if it's helpful:

Lord God, as we consider the way that your children around the world suffer, we ask you to speak to us about how we could respond.

After a moment of quiet, ask your group what they heard from God.

Place a cross – or a picture of Jesus on the cross – somewhere the group can see it, and then read these words from Revelation:

He will wipe all tears from their eyes, and there will be no more death, suffering, crying, or pain. These things of the past are gone forever. *(Revelation 21.4 CEV)*

CLOSING

Finish your time together with this prayer:

Lord God, who rejoices with those who rejoice and suffers with those who suffer, help us to seek you in all situations, looking for you at work in all things.

Amen.

PART 3
PREPARING FOR THE SERVICE

CHAPTER 1
THE ENROLMENT OF CONFIRMANDS

The enrolment of confirmands towards the start of their preparation was a new experience to me just a few years ago – but one I've really grown to love.

It's quite easy for the young people to be squirrelled away, preparing for their big day, and for the rest of the church to have no real idea who it is that's getting ready. By marking the start of the preparation with this simple liturgy, you not only set the preparation off on a good footing, you properly introduce the candidates to the rest of the church and call on them to pray for the young people as they prepare.

Furthermore, if you're involving young people confirmed in previous years with the preparation process, then they can present the current candidates to the church, thus taking their role as confirmed members of the adult congregation seriously.

There are several forms of this catholic liturgy around; this one was given to me by Revd Simon Leyshon, the former chaplain of Lord Wandsworth College in Hampshire. He assures me it's been cobbled together from a variety of sources – so please let me know if you think you deserve credit for any of it!

The liturgy gives you the opportunity to present the candidates with a Gospel – omit this section if necessary.

You may want to omit the intercessions or use them at a different time during your service.

There's a liturgy in *Common Worship* called the 'Call and Celebration of the Decision to be Baptized or Confirmed or to Affirm Baptismal Faith', if you fancy something more authorized. You can find this on www.churchofengland.org.[1]

RITE FOR THE ENROLMENT OF CANDIDATES

PRESENTATION

The Sponsors and Confirmands stand before the Priest.

Sponsors **We present to you these people of our community who wish to enter into a time of preparation, to receive the sacrament of confirmation.**

ACT OF COMMITMENT

The priest addresses the candidates.

Priest You are here to declare before me, and before members of your community, your intention to share in the life of the Holy Spirit through the sacrament of confirmation. I now ask you:

Are you prepared to commit yourself to a time of prayer and study so that you may understand more clearly the meaning of the sacrament you wish to receive?

Candidates **I am, with the help of the Holy Spirit**

Priest — Are you prepared to offer yourself, your time and your faith to serve your community in whatever way you can?
Candidates — **I am, with the help of the Holy Spirit**
Priest — Are you prepared to accept the call to witness to the presence of Christ among his people?
Candidates — **I am, with the help of the Holy Spirit**
Priest — Are you prepared to open your heart and mind so that the Holy Spirit may live within you?
Candidates — **I am, with the help of the Holy Spirit**

The priest addresses the sponsors and congregation.

Priest — Do you understand the gifts of the Spirit are given to us for the good of the whole Church?
All — **We do**
Priest — Do you therefore accept these members of your community as candidates for confirmation?
All — **We do**
Priest — Do you promise to share in their preparation for this sacrament by your prayers, your encouragement and your good example?
All — **We do**

ACCEPTANCE

Priest — May the faith and zeal you now have be with you and grow within you throughout your lives. I accept you as candidates for confirmation.
Candidates — **Thanks be to God**

PRESENTATION OF THE GOSPEL

Priest — Make the Gospel your constant study so that you may grow daily in the imitation of Christ.

INTERCESSIONS

Priest — Guided by the Holy Spirit, let us now pray to our heavenly Father, asking for those things that will enable us to live more fully the life of Christ.
Reader — For our community, that the witness and example of Christian life that we present to others may be an inspiration to them, and a source of faith and hope in their lives.
Lord, in your mercy
All — **Hear our prayer**
Reader — For all confirmands, that during their time of prayer and preparation their hearts and minds may be open and ready to accept the gifts of the Spirit.
Lord, in your mercy
All — **Hear our prayer**
Reader — For priests, catechists and sponsors who help confirmands with their preparation, that their minds and hearts may be filled with knowledge and understanding of the faith, and that the Spirit may guide them so that their word and example leads others to Christ.
Lord, in your mercy
All — **Hear our prayer**
Reader — For those who seek faith and for those who search for a meaning and value in life, that the Lord may come into their lives when they seek him with sincerity of heart, bringing them the consolation and hope that comes from knowing him and the good news of our salvation.
Lord, in your mercy
All — **Hear our prayer**
Priest — Lord Jesus Christ, Son of the living God, teach us to walk in your way more trustfully, to accept your truth more faithfully, and to share your life more lovingly.

By the power of the Holy Spirit, help us to live more generously as your disciples so that we may all come as one family to the kingdom of the Father where you live and reign for ever and ever.
All — **Amen**

CHAPTER 2
A PROGRAMME FOR A PRE-CONFIRMATION RETREAT

For the last five years I've had the privilege of helping to run the confirmation preparation for a school in the diocese in which I work. The chaplain had a tradition with his groups of taking them away each year on retreat the day before they were confirmed, to mirror the retreat ordinands go on before their ordination.

As I've led this retreat over the last few years I've used it as an opportunity to help young people develop further in their spirituality, but also to help them get a feel for the flow and shape of the confirmation service.

I've chosen a few key elements of the service and shaped activities for each section:

- Opening worship
- The preparation
- Liturgy of the Word
- Baptism
- Confession
- Intercessions
- Eucharist
- The blessing
- Closing prayer

Some of the ideas are taken from Jenny Baker's book, *Heart Soul Mind Strength*,[1] and are reproduced here with her kind permission.

OPENING WORSHIP

Gather the young people around a table and invite them to be still. Place a large candle on the table and read these words from John:

On the evening of that first day of the week, when the disciples were together, with the doors locked for fear of the Jewish leaders, Jesus came and stood among them and said, 'Peace be with you!' (John 20.19 NIV)

THE PREPARATION

TWENTY QUESTIONS[2]

You need one envelope and one sheet of questions for each pair of people in your group. Cut each sheet into thin strips, fold them and put them in an envelope.

Get people into pairs – you can decide whether you'll encourage people to join someone they don't know very well. Give each pair an envelope. One person draws out a question and asks it of their partner, who answers as honestly as they feel comfortably able. Conversations may develop from the questions, and the person who answers should feel free to ask the same thing of their questioner.

Allow about 20 minutes for this. Invite people to reflect on what they learned about each other.

- Who was your favourite Blue Peter presenter?
- What song would you sing at a karaoke evening?
- When did you last cry and why?

- Who cleans your toilet?
- If your best friend's wedding clashed with your mum's birthday party, which would you go to and why?
- What would you change about your church, if you could?
- If you had a one-to-one meeting with the Prime Minister, what would you talk about?
- Who is the most inspiring woman that you know?
- Have you ever shoplifted? Tell the story.
- Porridge, toast, or cereal for breakfast?
- What would you do if you weren't afraid?
- What do you hope you are doing in 10 years' time?
- What were you afraid of when you were five, and when did you stop fearing it?
- What does your inner critic say to you most often, and how do you respond?
- Imagine you could have a month's holiday anywhere in the world. Where would you go?
- When did you last do something that you have never done before?
- What colour is the inside of your head?
- Who are you looking forward to meeting in heaven?
- Which reality TV show would you most like to go on, or least like to, and why?
- What question were you most dreading?

Explain that over the course of the confirmation preparation you've spent a lot of time getting to know each other better – hopefully getting to know Christ better too. He once asked his disciples: 'Who do you say I am?' How would you answer that question today?

Allow some time for discussion.

LITURGY OF THE WORD

LECTIO DIVINA

Hopefully you're now used to the Lectio Divina method of reading the Bible. If not you can find instructions on page 24.

Use the method to read and discuss one of the readings that will be used in the confirmation service. If you can find out which passage the bishop will be preaching from, even better.

BAPTISM

EXAMEN[3]

The examen is an Ignatian exercise that invites us to look back over our day and ask two simple questions: For what moment am I most grateful? And for what moment am I least grateful?

You'll need:

- large sheets of paper
- pens
- a plate of lemon wedges
- a dish of breadsticks
- a bowl of honey.

Cut the lemons into slices and put them, the honey and the breadsticks in three separate dishes. On a large sheet of paper, write the word 'bitter' in the centre of one side and write the word 'sweet' in the centre of the other side. If you have a large group, you may need to prepare more sheets, so that a small group can gather round each. You'll start with the side that says 'sweet'.

Remind people that God is with them and that God loves them. Pray, thanking God for God's presence and asking God to help the group in this activity. You may feel it is appropriate to use a stilling exercise, to encourage the group to settle into God's presence.

Invite the young people to shut their eyes and think back over the last week. Get them to go over the things they've done, the people that they've spent time with, the places they've been. Encourage them to think about the different feelings they've experienced: the highs and lows of the last week. Allow a bit of time for this, and play some suitable music to help people to relax into it.

Then ask people to think about this question:

- For what moment in the last week am I most grateful?

Invite them to draw or write something on the sheet that represents this moment of gratitude. Invite them to eat some honey and breadsticks and thank God that God was with them in that moment. Invite them to consider what it was about that moment that was so special. What opportunity does it give them to grow?

Then turn the sheets over and invite people to think about the second question of the examen:

- For what moment in the last week am I least grateful?

Again, invite them to draw or write something on the sheet that represents this moment. Acknowledge that this question may raise uncomfortable feelings, but encourage them to stay with it. Invite them to eat a slice of lemon and to thank God that God was with them in that moment, even though they may not have been aware of that. Invite them to consider what it was about that moment that was difficult. What opportunity does it give them to grow?

Close this time with some prayer, or sung worship. Invite people to ask God how they should respond to those moments. Make sure that people know who they can talk to, if they need to take anything further.

CONFESSION

As your group reflect on the moments for which they were least grateful, they may want this to lead into a time of confession.

You might want to print out sheets with Psalm 51 on the left and blank or lined space on the right (see Figure 2). If you want to make your own version of this, an internet image search for 'notepaper' will give you lots of options. Encourage your group to find somewhere to sit quietly and to rewrite the psalm in their own words on the right-hand side. Once everyone has finished, invite anyone who wants to to share what they've written.

Figure 2 Psalm 51 exercise

INTERCESSIONS

OUTDOOR PRAYER[4]

A bit weather-dependent this, but well worth the effort if possible. There's something about getting outdoors that changes the way you feel and the way you can respond to God.

If there is not enough open space where you usually meet, take people to a park. If you want to do this in the winter instead, you could adapt these instructions and appropriate things that they can focus on.

Make enough copies of p. 101 for everyone to have one. Fold them up, from the bottom, along the lines, so that people can unfold them from the top, revealing one instruction at a time.

Gather everyone together and explain the activity. Tell them that they need to reveal instruction 1 in a moment and then follow it. Each time they have finished an instruction, they unfold the paper to reveal the next one. They read it and then take time to do what it says (rather than reading it trying to do it at the same time). Encourage them to linger on each instruction, not to rush through them.

ACTS

You'll need to give each of the members of your group a copy of the *i* newspaper (you can use any paper really, but I think the short articles in *i* work well with young people, not to mention that it only costs 20p!), four sheets of paper (one for each letter of ACTS), scissors and a glue stick.

Explain to them the concept of ACTS prayers: A – adoration, C – confession, T – thanksgiving and S – supplication.

Ask them to go through their newspapers and find stories and pictures that help them pray, and then to put them on their:

- **A**doration sheet – things that remind them of the awesomeness of God;
- **C**onfession sheet – things that make them want to say sorry for their or others' actions;
- **T**hanksgiving sheet – things that make them want to say thank-you to God;
- **S**upplication sheet – things that make them want to ask God for help.

Allow the group enough time to go through their newspapers and then bring them back together to see what they've each achieved.

EUCHARIST

PREPARATION OF THE TABLE

Once everyone has gathered again, you'll want to introduce the eucharistic section of the confirmation service. Have around the room the various things that you'll need to lay a table ready for a meal, and invite the group to collect and bring them to you one at a time. You'll need: a table cloth, a vase with some flowers, cutlery, a plate, a breadboard and a glass.

Carefully lay the table. You may want to do this quietly and reverentially.

THE EUCHARISTIC PRAYER

For this section you simply want to retell the story of the last supper, either reading it directly from one of the Gospels or telling it in your own words.

As you talk about the bread you should produce some bread (flat bread or pitta bread for authenticity) and place it on the breadboard, and when you talk about the wine you should produce a bottle of wine and pour it into the glass.

It's entirely up to you and your tradition whether or not you then share the wine and bread.

Once you've completed the activity, sit the group down and ask them these questions:

- Why do you think this act is so central for Christians?
- What do you think God might be saying to you through this activity?

THE BLESSING

Explain that this is it! Your confirmation preparation has finished and all that remains is for the group actually to be confirmed. Ask them how they feel. Nervous? Excited? A bit of both?!

Explain that you're going to finish your time together by blessing each other, by sharing a word of encouragement or prayer for each of the other members of the group. Give each of them a block of sticky notes and ask each of them to write a short word of encouragement or blessing for every other member of the group and then to stick the notes on their backs. Once everyone has finished they can peel their blessings off their backs and read them. You may want to suggest they take their blessings to the confirmation service in a pocket – to remind them of the time they've spent in preparation.

From experience, don't underestimate how long this activity will take. You may be surprised at the effort your group puts into encouraging each other.

CLOSING PRAYER

Finish with a closing prayer drawing your time together.

1 Find somewhere you can be in a space on your own, away from everyone else.

2 Lie down on your back. Place your hands flat on the floor. Take ten deep breaths, in and out, and feel yourself slowing down.

3 What can you hear? Listen carefully and name the sounds around you.

4 What noise is going on inside you? Name your worries, or the things on your mind, and imagine putting them to one side.

5 Sit and grow used to the silence around you, and ask God to meet you in it.

6 Find a leaf, a flower, or a blade of grass and take a close look at it.

7 Think about the creation around you: trees, flowers and grass growing and changing throughout the year, in silence. Imagine what this place looks like through the different seasons – winter, spring, summer and autumn.

8 The Bible says: 'The basic reality of God is plain enough. Open your eyes and there it is! By taking a long and thoughtful look at what God has created, people have always been able to see what their eyes as such can't see: eternal power, for instance, and the mystery of God's divine being' (Romans 1.19–20 THE MESSAGE). What does God's creation tell you about God?

9 God, the creator of this amazing world, knows and loves you in the deepest way possible. Spend some time thanking God for God's love, for God's care, for God's presence in your life. Then just rest in God's presence, enjoying God's love.

10 When you are ready, go back and join the others. But carry this still moment with you.

NOTES

PREFACE

1 Pete Maidment and Paul Butler, *Living Your Confirmation: Putting Promises into Action* (London: SPCK, 2012).

INTRODUCTION

1 There's a full working of the role of adolescent development and confirmation in chapter 3 of Pete Maidment and Susie Mapledoram, with Stephen Lake, *Reconnecting with Confirmation* (London: Church House Publishing, 2011).
2 http://peterrollins.net/?p=1254 (accessed 23 January 2013).
3 http://jasonclark.ws/post/35304508837/94-of-uk-young-people-will-never-find-faith-of-any (accessed 23 January 2013).
4 David Kinnaman, *You Lost Me: Why Young Christians Are Leaving Church... and Rethinking Faith* (Grand Rapids, MI: Baker Books, 2011), p. 192.
5 Kenda Creasy Dean, *Practicing Passion: Youth and the Quest for a Passionate Church* (Grand Rapids, MI: Eerdmans, 2004).
6 24-7 Prayer is a charity that exists to enable young people to pray. It is best known for popularizing the idea of running 24/7 prayer weeks, where churches set aside a space for a week and people use it to pray for the whole of that seven-day period. The charity has run prayer rooms in churches and schools, and even taken the concept to Ibiza for the summer clubbing season. You can find out more at http://uk.24-7prayer.com (accessed 23 January 2013).
7 Dean, *Practicing Passion*, p. 99 (italics in original).
8 Dean, *Practicing Passion*, p. 129.
9 The language of fidelity, transcendence and communion are taken from chapters 3–5 of Dean's excellent *Practicing Passion*. I suspect I've done a poor job of communicating her work and strongly recommend reading it directly!

PART 1

1 WHAT IS THE POINT OF CONFIRMATION?

1 Philip Fryar, 'Heaven and Hell', in *Through the Eyes of a Child: New Insights in Theology from a Child's Perspective*, ed. Anne Richards and Peter Privett (London: Church House Publishing, 2009), pp. 269–83.
2 David Kinnaman, *You Lost Me: Why Young Christians Are Leaving Church... and Rethinking Faith* (Grand Rapids, MI: Baker Books, 2011), pp. 92–3.
3 Kinnaman, *You Lost Me*, pp. 119, 123.
4 Douglas C. Kimmel and Irving B. Weiner, *Adolescence: A Developmental Transition* (New York and Chichester: Wiley, 1995).
5 There's much more detail on adolescent development in Pete Maidment and Susie Mapledoram, with Stephen Lake, *Reconnecting with Confirmation* (London: Church House Publishing, 2011).
6 General Synod of the Church of England, *On the Way: Towards an Integrated Approach to Christian Initiation* (London: Church House Publishing, 1995), p. 67.
7 Jean Piaget's *The Child's Conception of the World*, originally published in the first half of the twentieth century, is a seminal psychological text. For a brief overview of the formal operational stage referred to above, read this 1981 journal extract from the Association for Supervision and Curriculum Development – www.ascd.org/ASCD/pdf/journals/ed_lead/el_198110_day.pdf (accessed 29 November 2013).

2 WHAT DOES IT MEAN TO BE AN ADULT CHRISTIAN?

1 For a fuller explanation of this statement I would recommend reading chapters 3 and 4, in particular, of Pete Maidment and Susie Mapledoram, with Stephen Lake, *Reconnecting with Confirmation* (London: Church House Publishing, 2011).
2 Tony Morgan, *Developing a Theology of Leadership* (e-book, Tony Morgan Live, 2011).
3 Referenced in Christopher A. Beeley and Joseph. H. Britton, 'Introduction: Toward a Theology of Leadership', *The Anglican Theological Review* 91.1, 2009.
4 From Paul Moore, *Making Disciples in Messy Church* (Abingdon: Bible Reading Fellowship, 2013). Moore explains and develops the Engel scale.
5 Soul Survivor is an evangelical/charismatic festival for young people that runs each summer. It combines Bible teaching and prayer ministry with extended times of sung worship at which young people are typically encouraged to meet intimately with God. It's during this time of musical worship that many will experience God and be moved to respond in some way.
6 Grace Davie, *Religion in Britain Since 1945: Believing Without Belonging* (Oxford: Blackwell, 1994).
7 Kenda Creasy Dean, *Practicing Passion: Youth and the Quest for a Passionate Church* (Grand Rapids, MI: Eerdmans, 2004), p. 151 (italics in original).

3 A TYPICAL SESSION OUTLINE

1 Mark Yaconelli, *Helping Teenagers to Pray* (London: SPCK, 2009), pp. 39–40.
2 Yaconelli, *Helping Teenagers to Pray*, p. 40.
3 Sally Dakin, the author of *Praying with Stuff: Ideas for Hands-on Prayer* (Cambridge: Grove Books, 2008), offered this explanation in 'Living the Mission of Jesus', the Diocese of Winchester's 2014 Lent Course. The idea is to read the text very slowly, engaging deeply with God through his Word in four stages:

- **Read**: In a group, two or more people read the passage slowly and gently, while everyone listens expectantly for a word or phrase that engages them. They may be invited to speak out the word or phrase, without explanation.
- **Reflect**: People chew over the word or phrase in silence, absorbing it and internalizing its meaning. They may choose to speak out a sentence expressing the message they have received; there are no comments or discussion.
- **Respond**: Again in silence, people respond to the God who has spoken to them. They may wish to articulate a one-sentence prayer.
- **Rest**: Finally the group spend a few more minutes in silence, together enjoying the presence and the peace of the God who is Love.

4 http://en.wikipedia.org/wiki/Nonverbal_communication (accessed 23 October 2013).
5 Jenny Baker, *Heart Soul Mind Strength: 50 Creative Worship Ideas for Youth Groups* (Oxford: Monarch, 2008).

PART 2, SECTION 1

2 FELLOWSHIP

1 *Common Worship: Christian Initiation* (London: Church House Publishing, 2006), p. 119. *Common Worship: Christian Initiation* is copyright © The Archbishops' Council, 2006, and extracts are reproduced by permission. All rights reserved (copyright@churchofengland.org).
2 In 2007 the average age of worshippers in the Church of England was 61 (www.churchofengland.org/media/1032500/celebratingdiversitygsmisc938.pdf (accessed 2 July 2013), p. 38). Average life expectancy in the UK is 80.75 (www.google.co.uk/publicdata/explore?ds=d5bncppjof8f9_&met_y=sp_dyn_le00_in&hl=en&dl=en&idim=country:GBR:JPN:CHN (accessed 2 July 2013)).

3 BREAKING BREAD

1 Pete Maidment and Susie Mapledoram, with Stephen Lake, *Reconnecting with Confirmation* (London: Church House Publishing, 2011).
2 *Common Worship: Services and Prayers for the Church of England* (London: Church House Publishing, 2000), p. 185. Extracts from *Common Worship: Services and Prayers* are copyright © The Archbishops' Council, 2000, and are reproduced by permission. All rights reserved (copyright@churchofengland.org).
3 Icon Home Entertainment, 2000.

4 PRAYER

1 Pete Maidment and Paul Butler, *Living Your Confirmation: Putting Promises into Action* (London: SPCK, 2012).

5 RESISTING EVIL

1 From David Wilkerson, with John and Elizabeth Sherrill, *The Cross and the Switchblade* (New York: B. Geis Associates/ Random House, 1963; republished many times since). This chapter is available to read at http://shop.cbn.com/firstchapter.asp?mode=view&index=1432 (accessed 3 January 2014).

2 Jackie Pullinger's story can be found in Jackie Pullinger, with Andrew Quicke, *Chasing the Dragon* (London: Hodder & Stoughton, 1980; rev. edn 2006). A brief history of her work and a video of her talking about her calling is available at www.ststephenssociety.com (accessed 3 January 2014).

3 Stephen Tomkins, *The Clapham Sect: How Wilberforce's Circle Transformed Britain* (Oxford: Lion, 2010), p. 73.

4 *Common Worship:* New Patterns for Worship, Sample Services, 'Believe and Trust: Holy Communion with Baptism', p. 367 – see www.churchofengland.org/prayer-worship/worship/texts/newpatterns/sampleservicescontents/npw7.aspx (accessed 15 October 2013).

6 REPENT AND RETURN

1 Pete Maidment and Paul Butler, *Living Your Confirmation: Putting Promises into Action* (London: SPCK, 2012), pp. 71–2.

8 SEEK AND SERVE CHRIST IN ALL PEOPLE

1 *Common Worship: Christian Initiation* (London: Church House Publishing, 2006), p. 119. *Common Worship: Christian Initiation* is copyright © The Archbishops' Council, 2006, and extracts are reproduced by permission. All rights reserved (copyright©churchofengland.org).

2 Church of England Archbishops' Council Education Division/ The National Society, *Going for Growth: Transformation for Children, Young People and the Church*, GS 1769, January 2010, p. 9; available at www.churchofengland.org/media/59351/goingforgrowth.pdf (accessed 15 October 2013).

3 From her address to the United Nations in 1985.

9 ACKNOWLEDGE CHRIST'S AUTHORITY

1 Pete Maidment and Paul Butler, *Living Your Confirmation: Putting Promises into Action* (London: SPCK, 2012).

10 DEFENDING THE WEAK

1 Pete Maidment and Paul Butler, *Living Your Confirmation: Putting Promises into Action* (London: SPCK, 2012).

2 Maidment and Butler, *Living Your Confirmation*, pp. 111–14.

PART 2, SECTION 2

11 SEX

1 http://religion.blogs.cnn.com/2011/09/27/why-young-christians-arent-waiting-anymore/ (accessed 9 June 2014).

2 David Kinnaman, *You Lost Me: Why Young Christians Are Leaving Church . . . and Rethinking Faith* (Grand Rapids, MI: Baker Books, 2011), ch. 8.

3 Copyright © Kevin, Ana and Brian Draper, Steve Collins and Jonny Baker. This idea is borrowed from Labyrinth, created in 2000 by members of Grace, Epicentre and Live On Planet Earth alternative worship groups – www.labyrinth.org.uk (accessed 3 July 2013).

12 ALCOHOL

1 www.bbc.co.uk/news/education19870190 (accessed 10 June 2014).

13 IMAGE

1 www.retail-week.com/the-changing-face-of-fashion-retail/5037465.article (accessed 17 July 2013).

2 www.theguardian.com/music/2013/oct/03/sinead-o-connor-open-letter-miley-cyrus (accessed 17 July 2013).

14 EXAMS

1 www.prayerideas.org/wp/praying_for_needs/final-exam-prayer-using-Bible-verses/ (accessed 17 July 2013).

15 BUSYNESS

1 www.princes-trust.org.uk/about_the_trust/what_we_do/research/youth_index_2013.aspx (accessed 8 October 2013).

2 www.unicef.org.uk/Latest/Publications/Report-Card-11-Child-well-being-in-rich-countries/ (accessed 8 October 2013).

3 www.newscientist.com/article/mg21829130.100-why-teenagers-really-do-need-an-extra-hour-in-bed.html#.UlUkMiSsj9g (accessed 8 October 2013).
4 www.nhs.uk/Conditions/stress-anxiety-depression/Pages/ways-relieve-stress.aspx (accessed 8 October 2013). Reproduced by kind permission of the Department of Health, © 2014.

16 SEXUALITY

1 *Common Worship: Services and Prayers for the Church of England* (London: Church House Publishing, 2000), p. 175. Extracts from *Common Worship: Services and Prayers* are copyright © The Archbishops' Council, 2000, and are reproduced by permission. All rights reserved (copyright©churchofengland.org).

17 SCIENCE

1 David Kinnaman, *You Lost Me: Why Young Christians Are Leaving Church . . . and Rethinking Faith* (Grand Rapids, MI: Baker Books, 2011), p. 140.
2 Gary Thomas, *Sacred Pathways* (Grand Rapids, MI: Zondervan, 2010), p. 30.
3 www.goodreads.com/quotes/4419-science-is-not-only-compatible-with-spirituality-it-is-a (accessed 18 December 2013).
4 www.telegraph.co.uk/news/religion/7849563/Richard-Dawkins-interested-in-setting-up-atheist-free-school.html (accessed 18 December 2013).
5 http://en.wikipedia.org/wiki/General_Scholium (accessed 18 December 2013).
6 www.salon.com/2009/04/14/jane_goodall/ (accessed 20 June 2014).
7 Henry Margenau, Roy Abraham Varghese (eds), *Cosmos, Bios, Theos: Scientists Reflect on Science, God, and the Origins of the Universe, Life, and Homo Sapiens* (La Salle, IL: Open Court Publishing, 1992), p. 71.
8 http://creation.com/testing-god-killing-the-creator (accessed 20 June 2014).
9 Nancy K. Frankenberry (ed.), *The Faith of Scientists: In Their Own Words* (Princeton, NJ: Princeton University Press, 2008), p. 432.

18 PORNOGRAPHY

1 *Letting Children be Children: Report of an Independent Review of the Commercialisation and Sexualisation of Childhood by Reg Bailey* is the 2011 report of the 'Bailey Review' set up by the Coalition government. It explores the impact that a sexualized culture is having on children and is a good read on this topic – www.gov.uk/government/publications/letting-children-be-children-report-of-an-independent-review-of-the-commercialisation-and-sexualisation-of-childhood (accessed 30 December 2013). It's also worth reading *Bye Buy Childhood: A Report into the Commercialisation of Childhood* by the Mother's Union – www.muenterprises.org/wp-content/themes/byebuymu/files/bye_buy_childhood_report_pdf.pdf (accessed 30 December 2013).
2 This article from the BBC highlights some of the counter-arguments to the 'porn damages young people' argument www.bbc.co.uk/news/magazine-22987051 (accessed 30 December 2013).
3 The NSPCC offers statistics and advice about young people's internet use – see www.nspcc.org.uk/help-and-advice/for-parents/online-safety/advice-for-parents/what-parents-need-know_wda99629.html (accessed 30 December 2013).

19 SUFFERING

1 This activity is adapted from an idea in Jenny Baker (ed.), *You Fish Shoes: Connecting 30 Key Issues with Christian Faith for 14–18-year-olds* (Birmingham: Christian Education Publications, 2005).

PART 3

1 THE ENROLMENT OF CONFIRMANDS

1 A direct link is www.churchofengland.org/media/41171/ciritesontheway.pdf (accessed 4 January 2014).

2 A PROGRAMME FOR A PRE-CONFIRMATION RETREAT

1 Jenny Baker, *Heart Soul Mind Strength: 50 Creative Worship Ideas for Youth Groups* (Oxford: Monarch, 2008). Permission also sought from the publisher.
2 Baker, *Heart Soul Mind Strength*, p. 174.
3 Baker, *Heart Soul Mind Strength*, p. 137.
4 Baker, *Heart Soul Mind Strength*, p. 148.